RHYTHM

UPLIFTING QUOTES FROM THE
AFRICAN AMERICAN PERSPECTIVE

PAULA MICHELE ADAMS

BALBOA.PRESS

A DIVISION OF HAY HOUSE

Balboa Press books may be ordered through booksellers or by contacting:

Balboa Press
A Division of Hay House
1663 Liberty Drive
Bloomington, IN 47403
www.balboapress.com
844-682-1282

Because of the dynamic nature of the Internet, any web addresses or links contained in this book may have changed since publication and may no longer be valid. The views expressed in this work are solely those of the author and do not necessarily reflect the views of the publisher, and the publisher hereby disclaims any responsibility for them.

The author of this book does not dispense medical advice or prescribe the use of any technique as a form of treatment for physical, emotional, or medical problems without the advice of a physician, either directly or indirectly. The intent of the author is only to offer information of a general nature to help you in your quest for emotional and spiritual well-being. In the event you use any of the information in this book for yourself, which is your constitutional right, the author and the publisher assume no responsibility for your actions.

Any people depicted in stock imagery provided by Getty Images are models, and such images are being used for illustrative purposes only. Certain stock imagery © Getty Images.

Author Photo by TidQuan K. Grant, Platinum House Studios

Reprinted by arrangement with The Heirs to the Estate of Martin Luther King, Jr., c/o Writer's House as agent for the proprietor New York, NY.

"If you can't fly ..." Copyright © 1956 by Dr. Martin Luther King, Jr. Renewed © 1984 by Coretta Scott King.

"Darkness cannot drive out darkness ..." Copyright © 1963 by Dr. Martin Luther King, Jr. Renewed © 1991 by Coretta Scott King.

Maya Angelou name and quote used with permission of Caged Bird Legacy, LLC.

Print information available on the last page.

ISBN: 978-1-9822-5428-5 (sc)
ISBN: 978-1-9822-5430-8 (hc)
ISBN: 978-1-9822-5429-2 (e)

Library of Congress Control Number: 2020917039

Balboa Press rev. date: 09/22/2020

For my mother, Lena Bell Adams,
who inspired me every day of my life
and to whom I owe all of who I am and who I am still becoming.
Without you the sunshine is dimmer.
Rest in peaceful bliss, Ma.

For my dear siblings: Crystal, Dawn, Tiffany, PJ, and Eileen.
My heart beats stronger because of our close bond of love, loyalty,
and family. I could not exist without your presence in my life.

For Christina, Danielle, Twiggy Cheyenne, LeSean,
Kennedy, Reece, Nola, and Malachi.
May you all be bodacious enough to always
follow your hearts' dreams
and courageous enough to live in your personal truths.
Take the world by storm!

This goes out to the underdog
Keep on keeping at what you love
You'll find that someday soon enough
You will rise up, rise up, yeah

—Alicia Keys
American musician, singer, composer, actress, classically trained pianist

If there is a book that you want to read, but it hasn't been written yet, you must be the one to write it.

—Toni Morrison
American novelist, essayist, editor, teacher

CONTENTS

ACKNOWLEDGMENTS

There are so many people who have believed in me throughout my life when I did not always believe in myself. They believed in my abilities, my goals, my vision, and me as a positive woman. I would not be where I am today without their encouragement, support, and most of all, love. I adore each and every one of them. They know who they are.

In memory of my parents, Lena Bell Adams and Paul Michael Adams, who made me who I am. They taught me what it meant to be a strong, Black woman. They fostered my talents and supported me no matter what path I chose to take. They were exemplary parents as well as great friends to me. They are loved immensely and greatly missed. May they be together in heaven, loving each other as they did on earth.

To my true friends, my family: Michele Gilbert, Edward Taylor, Cheryl Harper-Eastmond, Larry Krumenacker, Karen Inniss-George, Erin Anderson, Fannie Ellen Lee, James DuBarry, Cassandra Charles-Gerst, and Daryll Rollins (rest in peace). Thank you for your honest and real friendship, which is exceedingly difficult to find. Your acceptance of my eccentricities means everything. You are my family, my ride-or-dies, and my life would not have evolved into what it is without your influence, your laughter, your friendship, and your love.

I would like to thank Twiggy Cheyenne Hamilton, Eileen Croce-Adams, and Michele Gilbert for keeping this endeavor a secret and for assisting me with polishing the finished product. Your discerning eyes, valid points, and blind support mean the world to me.

Tiffany Nicole Adams ... you are the most loving and giving person I have ever come into contact with. I cannot thank you enough for your belief in me and your never ending support. You are far more than a sister you are a great friend and I love you dearly. I appreciate you and all that you do to help me try to make my life all that I dream it can be. You are an angel on my shoulder, always with me no matter the distance. You are simply amazing, and you deserve everything! Without your stabilizing force in my life, I don't know what I'd do. Thank you for being you!

I would like to thank Angela (Angel) Lucas, Cedric Shine and Richard (Cardo) Wright for your much appreciated belief in my vision, for your kind words of support, and for being such positive examples of Black power, Black pride, and Black excellence. I am grateful for each of you.

I'd like to thank TidQuan Grant for your professionalism, wonderful eye as a photographer, excellence as a DJ, and for your positivity toward all my projects and visions. You are an extraordinary and talented young Black man who will do great things in this world.

To Ingrid Heffner and the staff at Blue Mountain Arts (SPS Studios), thank you for believing in my work and for being the first to publish my writing. You gave me the confidence and courage to follow my heart's dream, and I will be forever grateful.

To the entire staff at Balboa Press, thank you for holding my hand and walking me through the publishing process. As a first-time author, your professional support was greatly needed and appreciated. May you continue to do wonderful things for the writing community.

INTRODUCTION

Since childhood, quotes have been a great source of inspiration for me, uplifting me at my lowest times, teaching me valuable lessons, and heightening my innate joy. They are my self-help go-to's. I treat them as daily affirmations from extraordinary and ordinary people, just like you or me. They cover a vast array of topics with a wide range of opinions that I may or may not agree with. But that is the beauty of a quote; it is personal to each of us. And we identify with the quote on different levels and in various ways.

People of African ancestry have gifted us with numerous quotes that expose the injustices they have lived through. The valuable lessons they have learned through their history include—but are not limited to—slavery, Jim Crow, being set "free," the civil rights movement, the Black Lives Matter movement, as well as our current challenges. We have much to learn about their journeys and experiences. Their quotes are living examples of those long-lived provocations and victories, and we are the fortunate recipients of their viewpoints, knowledge, strategies, and wisdom.

It was important for me to compile a book of native African and African American quotes to share with the world because when I sought one out, there was none that I could locate. There is so much insight to be had from our past and present-day thought leaders, activists, politicians, entertainers, and everyday people. There is truth and inspiration in these words for every nationality, ethnicity, and race told from the native African and African American perspective.

Our perspective is rich in history, innovation, and power. I find it imperative to share these words of self-reflection with you all. I have prefaced each chapter with my opinion on the way Black and Brown people, like myself, have conquered many forms of oppression, systemic racism, and racial inequality. These are not sweeping generalizations. Rather, this is *my* take on life as a Black person living in America.

May you find the same joy I have found and be uplifted by the sentiments behind each quote. May they resonate with you for a lifetime.

CHAPTER 1

On Failing

We have all heard the age-old adage, "Nothing beats a failure but a try." Well, without trying there would never be failure, and there would never be success either. The fear of failure permeates our society, but I am not sure why we are so afraid of it. Following your passion to fruition fulfills the soul. Without that fulfillment, are you really living? Without some failures, is there even growth?

Much like the fear of rejection, the fear of failing often leads to remaining stagnant in your life. Instead of going out on faith and instinct, you reject the notion that you would actually be a success at whatever it is that you want to pursue. You therefore put the brakes on the idea altogether, and your dream is not realized. Nor are your goals met.

As a people, African Americans have been predisposed to failure since slavery. By being thought of as subpar and less than—less than intelligent, less than worthy, less than human, less than American— doors were not opened to us. And the road to success was paved with coal. After decades of attempting to fight our way through this racial bias, Black and Brown people still struggle with that fight. We are often deemed failures when we have not been granted the opportunity to be placed in the position to succeed, therefore failing before being given the chance to try.

The fear of failure has been ingrained in us since we were brought to this country. It is just another learned behavior. So *unlearn it*. The truth is that failure is a part of life, as is success. Failure is not necessarily a negative. It offers you the opportunity to learn, to expand your vision, and to begin again. To improve yourself and to approach your goal from a different vantage point. Failure gives you another chance to prove the naysayers, and yourself, wrong.

Nothing in life is guaranteed. Do not give up on yourself before you even try. Do not feel defeated before you put forth the effort to make this anticipated failure a success. Do not allow the anxiety associated with failing deter you from putting your best foot forward and showing what you have to contribute. No matter what the outcome, you are a success the moment you let go of the fear and put yourself in the game.

Kobe Bryant said, "If you're afraid to fail, then you're probably going to fail." Believe in yourself, and always bet on *you*. Do not allow the past to dictate your future. Sure, we were set up to fail from the beginning, but it is up to us to change that dynamic. You have it within yourself to accomplish all your goals, so go out there and live up to *your* expectations!

On Failing

➤ You may encounter many defeats, but you must not be defeated. In fact, it may be necessary to encounter the defeats, so you can know who you are, what you can rise from, how you can still come out of it.

~ **Maya Angelou** *(1928-2014)*
American poet, singer, memoirist, civil rights activist

➤ If there is no struggle there is no progress.

~ **Frederick Douglass** *(1818-1895)*
American social reformer, abolitionist, orator, writer, statesman

➤ Winning is great, sure, but if you are really going to do something in life, the secret is learning how to lose. Nobody goes undefeated all the time. If you can pick up after a crushing defeat, and go on to win again, you are going to be a champion someday.

~ **Wilma Rudolph** *(1940-1994)*
American Olympic track and field sprinter

➤ Don't sabotage your own greatness by succumbing to failure.

~ **Terri McMillan** *(1951)*
American author, known for the book turned movie, 'Waiting to Exhale'

➤ The reason people think it's important to be White is that they think it's important not to be Black.

~ **James Baldwin** *(1924-1987)*
American essayist, playwright, novelist, poet, voice of the American civil rights movement

➤ Think like a Queen. A Queen is not afraid to fail. Failure is another steppingstone to greatness.

> **~ Oprah Winfrey** (1954)
> *American media mogul, actress, talk show host,*
> *TV producer, billionaire philanthropist*

➤ Failure is a feeling before it becomes an actual result.

> **~ Michelle Obama** (1964)
> *American lawyer, University Administrator, author,*
> *former First Lady of the United States*

➤ Failure is not an option. Success is just a process.

> **~ Wale** (1984)
> *American rapper, singer, actor*

➤ Life's a test, mistakes are lessons, but the gift of life is knowing that you have made a difference.

> **~ Tupac Shakur** (1971-1996)
> *American rapper, actor*

➤ Just don't give up what you're trying to do. Where there is love and inspiration, I don't think you can go wrong.

> **~ Ella Fitzgerald** (1917-1996)
> *American Jazz singer, referred to as the 'First Lady of Song'*

➤ Once you know what failure feels like, determination chases success.

> **~ Kobe Bryant** (1978-2020)
> *American professional basketball player*

➤ You're not obligated to win. You're obligated to keep trying to do the best you can every day.

> **~ Marian Wright Edelman** (1939)
> *President and Founder of the Children's Defense Fund*

➤ I will not lose, for even in defeat, there's a valuable lesson learned, so it evens up for me.

~ **Jay-Z** *(1969)*
American rapper, songwriter, record producer, record
executive, entrepreneur, philanthropist, businessman

➤ I really don't think life is about the I-could-have-beens. Life is about the I-tried-to-do. I don't mind the failure, but I can't imagine that I'd forgive myself if I didn't try.

~ **Nikki Giovanni** *(1943)*
American poet, writer, commentator, educator

➤ We all get distracted, the question is, would you bounce back or bounce backwards?

~ **Kendrick Lamar** *(1987)*
American rapper, songwriter, record producer, singer

➤ It isn't the mountains ahead to climb that wear you down. It's the pebble in your shoe.

~ **Muhammad Ali** *(1942-2016)*
American professional boxer, activist, philanthropist

➤ You don't come to terms with something before you do it. It's only after you've done it that you realize, you know, maybe that wasn't the best thing to do. Sometimes you gotta fall down to know the feeling to get up.

~ **DMX** *(1970)*
American rapper, songwriter who released his debut album 'It's Dark and
Hell is Hot' in 1998 to both critical acclaim and commercial success

> I can accept failure. Everyone fails at something. But I can't accept not trying.

~ **Michael Jordan** *(1963)*
American former basketball player, played 15 seasons and
won 6 championships with the Chicago Bulls

> When adversity strikes, that's when you have to be the most calm. Take a step back, stay strong, stay grounded and press on.

~ **LL Cool J** *(1968)*
American rapper, record producer, actor, author, entrepreneur

> Life is not a spectator sport. If you're going to spend your whole life in the grandstand just watching what goes on, in my opinion you're wasting your life.

~ **Jackie Robinson** *(1919-1972)*
American professional baseball player, first African American to play
in Major League Baseball in the modern era, broke the color line
when he started at first base for the Brooklyn Dodgers in 1947

> The triumph can't be had without the struggle.

~ **Wilma Rudolph** *(1940-1994)*
A sickly child who wore a brace on her left leg and overcame her
disabilities to compete in the 1956 Summer Olympic Games

> Stumbling is not falling.

~ **Malcolm X** *(1925-1965)*
American Muslim minister and human rights activist

> A lot of leaders fail because they don't have the bravery to touch that nerve or strike that chord.

~ **Kobe Bryant** *(1978-2020)*
Played his entire 20 season professional basketball
career with the Los Angeles Lakers

➤ You just have to find that thing that's special about you that distinguishes you from all the others, and through true talent, hard work, and passion, anything can happen.

~ **Dr. Dre** *(1965)*
American rapper, songwriter, record producer, entrepreneur,
record executive, actor, audio engineer

➤ Refuse to give up, your mistakes don't define you. They don't dictate where you're headed, they remind you.

~ **T.I.** *(1980)*
American rapper, singer, actor, songwriter, producer,
entrepreneur, record executive, author

➤ The person who makes no mistakes is usually not making anything. No money, no forward progress, nothing!

~ **Charlamagne Tha God** *(1978)*
American radio presenter, TV personality, author

➤ Change will not come if we wait for some other person or some other time. We are the one's we've been waiting for. We are the change we seek.

~ **Barack Obama** *(1961)*
44th President of the United States (2009-2017)

➤ A setback is a setup for a comeback.

T. D. Jakes *(1957)*
American Clergyman, author, filmmaker, Bishop of The Potter's
House, a non-denominational American Megachurch

➤ Mistakes are part of life. It is the response to the error that counts.

~ **Nikki Giovanni** *(1943)*
A major force in the Black Arts Movement

➢ Mistakes are meant for learning, not to repeat the same decisions.

~ **Roddy Ricch** *(1998)*
American rapper, singer, songwriter

➢ We spend so much time being afraid of failure, afraid of rejection. But regret is the thing we should fear most.

~ **Trevor Noah** *(1984)*
South African comedian, writer, producer, political commentator, actor, television host

➢ Failure: Is it a limitation? Bad timing? It's a lot of things. It's something you can't be afraid of because you'll stop growing. The next step beyond failure could be your biggest success in life.

~ **Debbie Allen** *(1950)*
American actress, dancer, choreographer, singer, songwriter, director, producer, a former member of the President's Committee on the Arts and Humanities

CHAPTER 2

On Negativity

We are surrounded by so much negativity that it is difficult to remain positive. We experience it every day in society, in the media, and in politics. We are exposed to negativity with the police, in our schools, in our workplaces, and in our relationships. How can we, as a people, transcend the negative environment in which we live and not succumb to all the mind-numbing minutia that surrounds us on a daily basis?

When I watch a news story, without fail I am thinking, *Please, don't let them be Black*. I know I am not the only one. This is because negative images of the African American community inundate the media on a persistent and consistent basis. Its predominance seems unbalanced in comparison to all the good and progressive people in our community. I believe we are highlighted unfavorably at a disproportionate rate.

As any sane person knows, not all Black men are deadbeat fathers who are out robbing old ladies, raping women, selling drugs, or gangbanging. Not all Black women are single mothers with several baby daddies, who are milking the welfare system, shoplifting, or being beaten by a pimp. Why do these images permeate our news stories and society at such an alarming rate?

In my opinion, the predominant view of African Americans seems to be a negative one because the value, hardship, and inequality of the Black experience is simply not comprehended by much of White America. It seems as if many of them do not believe that our 401 years of oppression and systemic racism is a legitimate reality. While White privilege is real, I honestly believe that the large majority of White America denies its existence. They truly do not understand what its permanence means for our culture. Of course we have White allies, but from what I've witnessed, they are few and far between. I do not believe it is understood that the African American struggle has been real for centuries and is sadly still prevalent in the twenty-first century. The nonallies' belief appears to be that we reached the status of equal decades ago. We just need to get over the racism and oppression we have been forced to live with, and still continue to experience and fight against.

With the influx of the brutal slayings of innocent African American men and women across the country at the hands of White police officers, we have become enraged at losing our own at the hands of those who are given the responsibility of honorably enforcing law and order. What happened to "To serve and protect?" We have become more distrustful of the police now more than ever. We have taken to the streets in protest of such inhumane treatment and practices of these rogue officers who believe they are above the law. Change has to be made on national and federal levels to put an end to these blatant killings, to correct the lack of justice with the firing and successful prosecution of these officers, as well as a total reform of the policing system. Those in blue seem to be exempt from serious prosecution for these horrendous acts, which are not always exposed publicly. All ethnicities are now banding together in protest after protest across the nation, saying enough is enough. Change must come now. Black Lives Matter!

No matter how much good the Black community does, negative images of our people will always be prevalent. This, unfortunately, is the cross we have to bear. While we cannot change their minds, we can change *our* minds. We can forge ahead in full force and solidarity to prove them wrong. Most of all, we must choose not to let the negative portrayals wreak havoc within our souls and change us as a people. We have to always come from a place of positivity, no matter how difficult that may be to muster.

We all have people and situations in our lives that, in reality, *are* negative. We cannot ignore that fact. Do not allow the negative that is a part of your existence to become a hindrance to your essential growth. If you are in an unhealthy relationship, a negative work environment, or going through a challenging time, do something to change that circumstance for the better. Forward movement is your only recourse. That change is on you and no one else. Do not become a statistic. Do not live down to the racist view of you. Live up to your view of yourself and demonstrate that to the world. Do not let anyone or anything trample on your positive vibes by allowing it to become a negative influence in your life. Release that negativity into the universe, and grab hold of the power you have within to keep you moving on a positive path.

Remember, it is easy to put a negative spin on things. It is easy for Black people to be the scapegoats for all that is wrong in the world, instead of placing the blame across the board, where it belongs. That is their easy way out. When you allow them to take the easy way out, you invite the negative to take control. You are allowing them to win. *Don't*. Always stand up for who you are and what you believe in.

No matter what anyone says or does, you control your thoughts and actions. You know who you are and what you are not. Do not let one person's ignorance change you. Brush that energy off your shoulder and remain optimistic, even in the face of adversity. We must band together as a people, as a country, to end the negative stigma attached to being Black in America and demand the same rights as our White counterparts. We must stand up, speak up, and remain fervent in our continuing fight against the unfavorable portrayals we endure every day.

Looting and destroying our own communities are not the answers. I understand the anger and passion behind the need to fight against these injustices. I feel it too. But peaceful protests and holding people's feet to the fire are the ways to have our voices heard and our demands met. There is power in numbers. We cannot back down and allow our community to be silenced while we are simultaneously being wiped out by those who are supposed to stand for the law and restore order. Public Enemy said, "Our freedom of speech is freedom or death, we got to fight the powers that be." We can never stop fighting!

On Negativity

➤ It's bigger than Black and White. It's a problem with the whole way of life. It can't change overnight, but we gotta start somewhere.

~ **Lil Baby** *(1994)*
*American rapper, singer, songwriter, one of the most
prominent figures in the trap music scene*

➤ Never be limited by other people's limited imaginations.

~ **Dr. Mae C. Jemison** *(1956)*
*Former NASA Astronaut who became the first Black
woman to travel into space when she served as a mission
specialist aboard the Space Shuttle Endeavour*

➤ If you let a person talk long enough, you'll hear their true intentions. Listen twice, speak once.

~ **Tupac Shakur** *(1971-1996)*
Considered to be one of the most significant rappers of all time

➤ Surround yourself with only people who are going to lift you higher.

~ **Oprah Winfrey** *(1954)*
*Best known for hosting her own hugely popular internationally
syndicated talk show from 1986-2011*

➤ One of the lessons that I grew up with was to always stay true to yourself and never let what somebody else says distract you from your goals. And so, when I hear about negative and false attacks, I really don't invest any energy in them because I know who I am.

~ **Michelle Obama** *(1964)*
First African American First Lady of the United States

➤ No temporary chaos is worth your sanity.

~ **Nas** *(1973)*
American rapper, songwriter, entrepreneur, investor

➤ The important thing is to realize that no matter what people's opinions may be, they're only just that – people's opinions. You have to believe in your heart what you know to be true about yourself. And let that be that.

~ **Mary J. Blige** *(1971)*
American singer, songwriter, actress, philanthropist

➤ If you want it, and the more you keep hearing you can't have it, you just go and get it.

~ **Cardi B** *(1992)*
American rapper, songwriter, TV personality, actress

➤ The future rewards those who press on. I don't have time to feel sorry for myself. I don't have time to complain. I'm going to press on.

~ **Barack Obama** *(1961)*
A member of the Democratic Party, he was the first African-American President of the United States

➤ The price of hating other human beings is loving oneself less.

~ **Eldridge Cleaver** *(1935-1998)*
American writer, political activist

➤ You always hear 'Black Republican' but you never hear 'White Democrat.' We've got to get beyond the labels and stereotypes. Other people have hang-ups. I don't.

~ **J. C. Watts** *(1957)*
American politician, clergyman, athlete

➤ Everything negative – pressure, challenges – is all an opportunity for me to rise.

~ **Kobe Bryant** *(1978-2020)*
The only player in the NBA league's history to have two jersey numbers
retired with the same team, going from #8 to #24 midway through his career

➤ 'Cause I'm Black and I'm proud, I'm ready and hyped plus I'm amped. Most of my heroes don't appear on no stamps.

~ **Chuck D** *(1960)*
American rapper, author, producer

➤ In this day and age, especially with all the media and television, social media, and the internet, we are constantly being compared and comparing ourselves to others' lives and journeys. Keep your eyes on your own road.

~ **Sanaa Lathan** *(1971)*
American actress, voice actress

➤ It's not the load that breaks you down, it's the way you carry it.

~ **Lena Horne** *(1917-2010)*
American singer, dancer, actress, civil right activist

➤ In a world filled with hate, we must still dare to hope. In a world filled with anger, we must still dare to comfort. In a world filled with despair, we must still dare to dream. And in a world filled with distrust, we must still dare to believe.

~ **Michael Jackson** *(1958-2009)*
American singer, songwriter, dancer, dubbed the 'King of Pop,'
regarded as one of the greatest entertainers of all time

➢ As a Black man, sometimes you can't tell if what you're seeing has underlying bigotry, or it's a normal conversation and you're being paranoid. That dynamic in itself is unsettling. I admit sometimes I see race and racism when it's not there.

*~ **Jordan Peele** (1979)*
American actor, comedian, writer, director, producer, best known for his television work in the comedy and horror genres

➢ I did what they said I couldn't. Went where they said I wouldn't.

*~ **2 Chainz** (1977)*
American rapper, songwriter, basketball player, media personality

➢ Me only have one ambition, Y'know. I only have one thing I really like to see happen. I like to see mankind live together – Black, White, Chinese, everyone – that's all.

*~ **Bob Marley** (1945-1981)*
Jamaican singer, songwriter, musician

➢ They talk about God, family, and country, but it's God until it's about poor people, it's family until family is same-sex and inclusive, and country until it involves Black people.

*~ **DeRay Mckesson** (1985)*
American civil rights activist, podcast host, former school administrator

➢ It is not our differences that divide us. It is our inability to recognize, accept and celebrate those differences.

*~ **Audre Lorde** (1934-1992)*
American writer, feminist, womanist, librarian, poet, civil rights activist

➤ It's one thing when other African Americans try to threaten my race card, but when people outside of my ethnicity have the audacity to question how 'down' I am because of the bleak, stereotypical picture pop culture has painted for me as a Black woman? Unacceptable.

~ Issa Rae *(1985)*
Senegalese-American actress, writer, producer, author

➤ There are many, many communities, many ethnic minorities, many civilizations that have been brutalized by others and you have to move on. You cannot perpetually stay in that place of blame, otherwise it's just a downward spiral.

~ David Oyelowo *(1976)*
English-American actor, producer

➤ If they don't give you a seat at the table, bring a folding chair.

~ Shirley Chisolm *(1924-2005)*
American politician, educator, author

➤ Hate is too great a burden to bear. It injures the hater more than it injures the hated.

~ Coretta Scott King *(1927-2006)*
American author, activist, civil rights leader

➤ If we accept and acquiesce in the face of discrimination, we accept the responsibility ourselves. We should, therefore, protest openly everything … that smacks of discrimination or slander.

~ Mary McLeod Bethune *(1875-1955)*
American educator, stateswoman, philanthropist,
humanitarian, womanist, civil rights activist

➤ People warn me, when you're on top there's envy.

~ Nas *(1973)*
Made a huge impact in the early 1990's with his album 'Illmatic,'
widely regarded as one of the greatest rap albums of all time

➤ There are times in life when, instead of complaining, you do something about your complaints.

~ Rita Dove *(1952)*
American poet, author, essayist

➤ You can kill a man, but you can't kill an idea.

Medgar Evers *(1925-1963)*
American civil rights activist in Mississippi, the state's Field Secretary for the NAACP, World War II veteran who served in the United States Army. Assassinated in 1963

➤ It ain't where you're from, it's where you're at.

~ Rakim *(1968)*
American rapper

➤ The soul that is within me no man can degrade.

~ Frederick Douglass *(1818-1895)*
After escaping from slavery in Maryland, he became a national leader of the abolitionist movement in Massachusetts and New York

➤ Negative people can only infest you with discouragement when they find you around ... just get lost and get saved!

~ Israelmore Ayivor
Inspirational writer, blogger, life skills entrepreneur

➤ Black people are apparently responsible for calming the fears of violent cops in the way women are supposedly responsible for calming the sexual desires of male rapists.

~ Ibram X. Kendi *(1982)*
American author, historian who recently joined Boston University to launch the BU Center for Antiracist Research

➤ The Black skin is not a badge of shame, but rather a glorious symbol of national greatness.

~ Marcus Garvey *(1887-1940)*
Jamaican political activist, publisher, journalist, entrepreneur, orator

➤ Most people don't want to change. They're comfortable and set in their ways. But in order to change, you have to be able to agitate people at times. And I think that's something that's very necessary for us to improve as a country.

~ Colin Kaepernick *(1987)*
American civil rights activist, football quarterback who is a free agent

➤ I'm a Black man in the United States of America, so I always feel like there's a target on me.

~ Wale *(1984)*
His song 'Breakdown' was featured on the video game Madden NFL 2009

➤ God doesn't judge dark skin; he judges dark hearts.

~ Unknown

CHAPTER 3

On the Value of Hard Work

In life, nothing worth having comes easy. That is not just a cliché; it's a fact. As difficult as it may be to admit, many of us do not reach our goals because we do not put forth the time and effort required to obtain them. It is as if we believe that thinking of the goal will manifest it into being. Well, I am sure we both know that is the furthest thing from the truth.

Setting a goal and sitting on it, waiting for it to happen without your passionate reinforcement, is a waste of your time and your life. Setting small, attainable goals is often the first step to making your dreams come true. You must then follow through and put forth extra energy and hard work to meet each deadline. This is the key to reaching your ultimate goal.

Many of us find excuses as to why we haven't "arrived," why we have fallen short of the vision we have for ourselves and our lives. If you look deeply into yourself, the answer is just below the surface. The answer is *you*. What have you done today to achieve your goals? What active work have you begun to set you on the path to success? Just thinking about it does nothing to get you to where you need—or want—to be. An idea without purpose is just a fleeting thought. Make that idea a reality.

There are twenty-four hours in each day. How many of those hours are you actively working, outlining, researching, and fighting for your future? How many of those hours are you chillin', hanging out, playing video games, or sleeping? The answers to those questions factor into why you may not be where you want to be on your journey.

Excelling and achieving come down to one thing—hard work. You need a dedicated, persistent work ethic. You have to literally do what you have to do until you start to see the fruits of your labor being born. Sometimes it takes knocking on hundreds of doors until someone opens one of them. Sometimes it takes working three jobs to fund your dream. Sometimes it takes going out of your comfort zone and asking for assistance from those wiser and more experienced than yourself. Sometimes you have to create a new path. No matter how you go about it, hard work and discipline are essential in reaching your goal. Luck is a figment of your imagination. Hard work is the key to getting where you need and want to be. It is your only concrete way up the ladder to success.

It is still said that African Americans have to work twice as hard to achieve half the success and pay as our Caucasian counterparts. With that reality in your mind, what are you doing today to be able to stand at the same level of the podium or higher than our counterparts? If you are resting on your laurels and not putting in the work, you are destined to fall short of your goal.

There is honor and value in hard work. So many young people in the past couple of generations have come to feel entitled, believing that everything is owed to them and they should not have to work hard for anything. Untrue, untrue, untrue. There are no forty acres and a mule waiting for you. There is only hard work. Nothing is going to fall into your lap, and if it does, your lap best be prepared for any opportunity that may reveal itself. Preparation meeting opportunity is key to success. You must seize each opportunity that is bestowed upon you if you are going to excel in this competitive and unequal world.

Reparations will not come. So if you haven't already done so, get up right now and begin putting forth the effort required to reach your goals. Don't put off for tomorrow what can be done today. Set yourself up for success by working your ass off until you cannot work anymore. Do the work and reap the reward. Remember the value of hard work and make the moves necessary to change your life for the better today.

Do not feel defeated by the racist world we live in. Pave your own way. You can achieve great things despite the roadblocks put in your way by a system that does not always embrace our exemplary contributions. It is up to you to challenge yourself, to push yourself past your comfort level and ring that bell at the peak of your goal so that you can move on to your next goal. Do not languish in the difficulties that you may face. Press on and continue to put forth your best effort at everything you do. Believe in yourself, trust the process, and do not wait until tomorrow. Seize the day!

On the Value of Hard Work

➤ If you can't fly then run, if you can't run then walk, if you can't walk then crawl, but whatever you do you have to keep moving forward.

> **~ Dr. Martin Luther King, Jr.** *(1929-1968)*
> *American Christian minister and activist who became the most visible spokesperson and leader in the civil rights movement from 1955 until his assassination in 1968, known for his "I Have a Dream" speech*

➤ Ben Carson said Black people worked for less. I have breaking news: we built this joint for free. We didn't build it for less.

> **~ Angela Rye** *(1979)*
> *American attorney, a liberal commentator on CNN, NPR strategist, served as the general counsel to the Congressional Black Caucus for the 112th Congress*

➤ You don't make progress by standing on the sidelines.

> **~ Shirley Chisolm** *(1924-2005)*
> *In 1968, she became the first Black woman elected to the U.S. Congress representing New York for 7 terms: 1969-1983*

➤ Dreams are lovely, but they are just dreams. Fleeting, ephemeral, pretty. But dreams do not come true just because you dream them. It's hard work that makes things happen. It's hard work that creates change.

> **~ Shonda Rimes** *(1970)*
> *American television producer, television & film writer, author*

➤ If you're walking down the right path and you're willing to keep walking, eventually you'll make progress.

> **~ Barack Obama** *(1961)*
> *American attorney, community organizer*

➤ I'm not afraid of dying, I'm afraid of not trying.

> **~ Jay-Z** *(1969)*
> *First rapper to be inducted into the Songwriters Hall of Fame in 2017*

➤ Have a vision of excellence, a dream of success, and work like hell.

> **~ Dr. Samuel DuBois Cook** *(1928-2017)*
> *American political scientist, professor, author,*
> *administrator, human rights activist, civil servant*

➤ Until you dig a hole, you plant a tree, you water it and make it survive, you haven't done a thing. You are just talking.

> **~ Wangari Maathai** *(1940-2011)*
> *Kenyan environmental political activist, Nobel laureate*

➤ You can't just sit there and wait for people to give you that golden dream. You've got to get out there and make it happen for yourself.

> **~ Diana Ross** *(1944)*
> *American singer, actress, record producer*

➤ If you quit every time things don't go your way, then you'll be quitting all through your life.

> **~ Evander Holyfield** *(1962)*
> *American former professional boxer, competed from 1984–2011*

➤ Once a person is determined to help themselves, there is nothing that can stop them.

> **~ Nelson Mandela** *(1918-2013)*
> *President of South Africa from 1994-1999*

➤ I used to want the words 'She tried' on my tombstone. Now I want 'She did it.'

> **~ Katherine Dunham** *(1909-2006)*
> *American dancer, choreographer, author, educator, anthropologist, social activist*

➢ Developing a good work ethic is key. Apply yourself at whatever you do, whether you're a janitor or taking your first summer job, because that work ethic will be reflected in everything you do in life.

~ **Tyler Perry** *(1969)*
American actor, director, playwright, filmmaker, comedian, film studio owner

➢ Work hard, sleep less.

~ **Idris Elba** *(1972)*
British actor, producer, musician, DJ, rapper

➢ You have to be able to accept failure to get better.

~ **LeBron James** *(1984)*
American professional basketball player for the Los Angeles Lakers, widely considered to be one of the greatest basketball players in NBA history

➢ Whenever I feel bad, I use that feeling to motivate me to work harder. I only allow myself one day to feel sorry for myself. When I'm not feeling my best, I ask myself, "What are you going to do about it?" I use the negativity to fuel the transformation into a better me.

~ **Beyonce Knowles** *(1981)*
American singer, songwriter, actress, record producer, dancer, former lead vocalist of the R&B group Destiny's Child

➢ You never know which experiences of life are going to be of value … you've got to leave yourself open to the hidden opportunities.

~ **Robin Roberts** *(1960)*
American television broadcaster, anchor of ABC's Good Morning America, sportscaster on ESPN for 15 years

➢ Challenges make you discover things about yourself that you never really knew. They're what make the instrument stretch, what makes you go beyond the norm.

~ **Cicely Tyson** *(1924)*
American actress, former fashion model

➢ So, if diva means giving your best, then yes, I'm a diva.

~ **Patti Labelle** *(1944)*
American singer, actress, entrepreneur

➢ Stay positive but stay focused. Sometimes things can distract you and you don't want to be distracted on the journey to that mountain top.

~ **DJ Khaled** *(1975)*
American DJ, record executive, songwriter, record producer, author, media personality

➢ Success is to be measured not so much by the position that one has reached in life as by the obstacles which he has overcome while trying to succeed.

~ **Booker T. Washington** *(1856-1915)*
American educator, author, orator

➢ The vision will pull you forward, but you must nurture it.

~ **Iyanla Vanzant** *(1953)*
American lawyer, author, life coach, television personality

➢ There's always something to suggest that you'll never be who you wanted to be. Your choice is to take it or keep on moving.

~ **Phylicia Rashad** *(1948)*
American actress, singer, stage director, dubbed 'Mother of The Black Community' at the 2010 NAACP Awards

➢ The harder you work, the luckier you get.

~ **Mike Adenuga** *(1953)*
Nigerian billionaire businessman, second richest person in Africa

➢ I had to make my own living and my own opportunity. But I made it! Don't sit down and wait for the opportunities to come. Get up and make them.

~ **Madame C.J. Walker** *(1867-1919)*
American entrepreneur, philanthropist, political and social activist, recorded as the first female self-made millionaire in the Guinness Book of World Records

➢ As long as I keep working hard, the sky will be the limit.

~ **Andre Iguodala** *(1984)*
American professional basketball player for the Miami Heat, was an NBA All-Star in 2012 and has been named to the NBA All-Defensive Team twice

➢ I'm not going to continue knocking on that old door that doesn't open for me. I'm going to create my own door and walk through that.

~ **Ava Duvernay** *(1972)*
American filmmaker, film distributor, first Black woman to win the U.S. Dramatic Competition at the Sundance Film Festival in 2012

➢ Life has abundant treasures when your settings are on right.

~ **Donnie Simpson** *(1954)*
Long time American radio DJ, television, and movie personality

➢ Before Black Lives Matter, there was a dormancy in our Black freedom movement. Obviously, many of us were doing work, but we've been able to reignite a whole entire new generation, not just inside the U.S. but across the globe, centering Black people and centering the fight against White supremacy.

~ **Patrisse Cullors** *(1984)*
American artist, activist, advocate for prison abolition, co-founder of the Black Lives Matter movement

➢ Start working your plan today to set yourself free tomorrow.

~ Michael Baisden *(1963)*
American nationally syndicated radio personality,
host of the Michael Baisden Show

➢ What I really feel is necessary is that the Black people in this country will have to upset this apple cart. We can no longer ignore the fact that America is not the land of the free and the home of the brave.

~ Fannie Lou Hamer *(1917-1977)*
American voting activist, women's rights activist, community
organizer, a leader in the civil rights movement

➢ When it is time for you to leave this school, leave your job, or even leave this earth, you make sure you have worked hard to make sure it mattered you were even here.

~ Wes Moore *(1978)*
American author, social entrepreneur, television producer

➢ I'm grateful to see my work flourish in my lifetime. Many of the great people in our history were not able to see how much their work, suffering and sacrifices enriched our lives and pushed our struggle forward. But I've been blessed to see my work begin in a family home, spread around the world, and be embraced by millions of African people throughout the world African community.

~ Maulana Karenga *(1941)*
American professor of Africana Studies, activist, author, best known as the
creator of the Pan-African and the African American holiday of Kwanzaa

➢ Education is our passport to the future, for tomorrow belongs to the people who prepare for it today.

~ El Hajj Malik El Shabazz *(1925-1965)*
Malcolm X, a major proponent of the Black
Nationalism and Pan Africanism movements

➢ You face your greatest opposition when you're closest to your biggest miracle.

~ T.D. Jakes *(1957)*
He was "called" to preach at the age of 17, not knowing that his ministry would reach the entire nation and effect millions of people through books, radio, television, and conferences

➢ I know that I'm doing something right. I know other people see what I'm doing is right. It's something that we have to come together, we have to unite, we have to unify and make a change.

~ Colin Kaepernick *(1987)*
Played six seasons for the San Francisco 49ers, began his sitting protest against police violence during the San Francisco preseason games in support of those groups trying to effect change

➢ We are the people next door. All we have to do is open the door.

~ Tamron Hall *(1970)*
American broadcast journalist, television talk show host who won a Daytime Emmy Award for her first season of the Tamron Hall Show in 2020

➢ Not everything that is faced can be changed, but nothing can be changed until it is faced.

~ James Baldwin *(1924-1987)*
His first novel, "Go Tell It on the Mountain," published in 1953, was a loosely autobiographical tale focused on the life of a young man growing up in Harlem grappling with father issues and his religion

CHAPTER 4

On Being Happy

Like many Americans, I have suffered from depression most of my life. It is a daily struggle for me to find an inner happy place because darkness often takes over, and I find myself feeling anxious, sad, or melancholy for no outward reason.

There is a stigma in the African American community, especially with men, against mental health assistance; some believe it shows weakness. Mental health is supposed to be an issue that is handled within the four walls of our home—meaning it's nobody's business. This is a misunderstanding for much of our community.

Happiness comes from within. If you are battling conflict within your own mind, how can you be happy without assistance? Help comes in all forms: a mental health professional, a self-help book, inspirational quotes, a candid talk with a trusted friend, watching a comedy, listening to music; the list goes on. It is important to remember that there is no one way to get help, and there is no shame in seeking help. You are doing it for you and for your best good.

Many of us seek happiness from outside sources. We depend on them to fulfill the unhappiness we feel inside and make us all better. We often believe that happiness only comes with having money, a partner, or an upscale job; being a size 4; eating a pint of ice cream; and so on. None of these things define happiness. They may add to the overall happiness you feel in the moment, but they are like a bandage that covers up the unhappiness festering within.

Happiness is a choice. Choose happy every day. Look deeply within yourself and define what truly brings you joy. One of the most joyous moments I have is when I am spending time with my four-year-old twin niece and nephew. They are happiness personified for me. Music in all its forms is another source of happiness for me, so I regularly seek it out. Seeing the fruits of my labor makes me happy beyond belief because it means I have put in the work to achieve a much-sought-after goal. Loving and being loved bring me happiness. The beauty of nature brings me joy. Every day I attempt to find something new to look forward to that makes me happy or brings me joy.

The world can be a dark place. It is up to each of us to live in our truths, define what happiness means to us, and identify what truly puts smiles on our faces and joy in our hearts. No one can do that for us, so do not look for true happiness outside yourself. Happiness comes from within. Seek it from within. Define it. Enjoy it. And if you cannot, seek the help that is best for you.

Our ancestors fought and died to be free enough to make comfortable lives for themselves. Think of their struggles and what they survived for us to be able to have the lives we have today. We owe it to them to find some inner peace, joy, and true happiness every day we draw breath on this earth.

Live in the moment and have gratitude. Find your happy place and go there often. Happiness is a state of mind. Choose happy!

On Being Happy

➢ If you are unhappy with anything – whatever is bringing you down – get rid of it. Because you will find that when you are free, your true creativity, your true self comes out.

~ Tina Turner *(1939)*
Award winning singer and actress originally from the
United States and now a Swiss citizen

➢ To appreciate the sun you gotta know what rain is.

~ J. Cole *(1985)*
American rapper, singer, songwriter, producer, record executive

➢ I am not tragically colored. There is no great sorrow dammed up in my soul, nor lurking behind my eyes. I do not mind at all.

~ Zora Neale Hurston *(1891-1960)*
American author, anthropologist, filmmaker

➢ Life is short, and it's up to you to make it sweet.

~ Sadie Delany *(1889-1999)*
American educator, civil rights pioneer

➢ Life's impermanence, I realized, is what makes every single day so precious. It's what shapes our time here. It's what makes it so important that not a single moment is wasted.

~ Wes Moore *(1978)*
Decorated U.S. Army combat veteran

➢ Sometimes the best things are right in front of you; it just takes some time to see them.

~ Gladys Knight *(1944)*
American singer, songwriter, actress, author, businesswoman

➢ That's a big gift when people say to you that a song helped them or brought them to some place in their life where they needed to be.

~ Lenny Kravitz *(1964)*
American singer, songwriter, multi-instrumentalist, record producer, actor

➢ Life is all there is. And if that's true, then we have to really live it – we have to take it for everything it has and "die enormous" instead of "living dormant."

~ Jay-Z *(1969)*
First hip-hop artist to become a billionaire

➢ I am convinced that the Black man will only reach his full potential when he learns to draw upon the strengths and insights of the Black woman.

~ Manning Marable *(1950-2011)*
American professor of public affairs, history, and African American studies at Columbia University, active in progressive political causes

➢ There's not enough said about the beauty of being able to focus on what you do well.

~ Kimberly Bryant *(1967)*
American electrical engineer, Founder of 'Black Girls Code,' a training course that teaches basic programming concepts to Black girls who are underrepresented in technology careers

➢ Living in the moment means letting go of the past and not waiting for the future. It means living your life consciously, aware that each moment you breathe is a gift.

~ Oprah Winfrey *(1954)*
In 2011, she launched her own television network, the Oprah Winfrey Network (OWN)

➤ One of the hardest things in life is having words in your heart that you can't utter.

~ James Earl Jones *(1931)*
American actor, known for his performance in film, theater, and television, described as "one of America's most distinguished and versatile" actors

➤ A good head and a good heart are always a formidable combination.

~ Nelson Mandela *(1918-2013)*
South African anti-apartheid revolutionary, political leader, philanthropist

➤ Sometimes I would almost rather have people take away years of my life than take away a moment.

~ Pearl Bailey *(1918-1990)*
American actress, singer who won a Tony Award in 1968 for the all Black version of 'Hello Dolly'

➤ I'm happiest when I'm with young people. Their wisdom, grief, and optimism motivates me to work harder.

~ Lateefah Simon *(1977)*
American President of the Akonadi Foundation, an advocate for civil rights and racial justice, the youngest woman to receive a MacArthur Fellowship

➤ If you have the opportunity for your art to meet activism, you shouldn't pass that up when it comes your way.

~ Regina King *(1971)*
American actress, director, the recipient of an Academy Award, a Golden Globe Award and three Primetime Emmy Awards

➤ Being happy doesn't mean everything's perfect, it just means you've decided to look beyond the imperfections.

~ Reverend Run *(1964)*
American rapper, producer, DJ, television personality

➤ You are on the eve of a complete victory. You can't go wrong. The world is behind you.

~ Josephine Baker *(1906-1975)*
American-born French entertainer, French Resistance agent, civil rights activist

➤ When you are kind to someone in trouble, you hope they'll remember and be kind to someone else. And it'll become like wildfire.

~ Whoopi Goldberg *(1955)*
American actor, comedian, author, television personality

➤ No matter how bad things are, you can at least be happy that you woke up.

D. L. Hughley *(1963)*
American actor, political commentator, radio host, stand-up comedian

➤ Creation is everything you do. Make something.

~ Ntozake Shange *(1948-2018)*
American playwright, poet, Black feminist, best known for her Obie Award winning play 'For Colored Girls Who Have Considered Suicide/When the Rainbow is Enuf'

➤ You can't have a relationship with other people until you give birth to yourself.

~ Sonia Sanchez *(1934)*
Has authored over a dozen books of poetry, as well as short stories, critical essays, plays and children's books

➤ I try to keep focused on the things that really make me happy and just do those same things.

~ John Singleton *(1968-2019)*
American film director, screenwriter, producer, actor, best known for directing 'Boyz in the Hood,' for which he was the first African American and youngest person, at 24, to be nominated for an Academy Award for Best Director

➢ Be driven, be focused, but enjoy every moment because it happens only once.

~ **Alicia Keys** *(1981)*
American musician, singer, songwriter, composer, record
producer, actress, poet, author, entrepreneur, activist

➢ Don't wait around for other people to be happy for you. Any happiness you get you've got to make for yourself.

~ **Alice Walker** *(1944)*
American novelist, short story writer, poet

➢ Give light and people will find the way.

~ **Ella Baker** *(1903-1986)*
American civil rights activist, human rights activist

➢ You are the designer of your destiny; you are the author of your story.

~ **Lisa Nichols**
American motivational speaker, a featured teacher in 'The Secret,' Founder
of Motivating the Masses, CEO of Motivating the Teen Spirit, LLC

➢ We are all gifted. That is our inheritance.

~ **Ethel Waters** *(1896-1977)*
American singer, actress

➢ I try not to get too high off the highs or too low off the lows.

~ **Sterling K. Brown** *(1976)*
American actor, won a Primetime Emmy Award for
Outstanding Lead Actor in a Drama Series

➢ I don't think about other people. They are not walking in my shoes. They are not paying my bills. What makes me happy is when I do what I like to do, for me.

~ **Taraji P. Henson** *(1970)*
American actress, author

➢ Making people laugh is giving, and it's healing, too.

> **~ Chris Tucker** *(1971)*
> *American actor, stand-up comedian*

➢ In every life we have some trouble, but when you worry you make it double. Don't worry. Be happy.

> **~ Bobby McFerrin** *(1950)*
> *American Jazz vocalist*

➢ I don't mean to be facetious, but humor is the key to the soul.

> **~ Martin Lawrence** *(1965)*
> *American stand-up comedian, actor, producer, talk show*
> *host, writer, former Golden Gloves boxer*

➢ Just be honest and true to yourself. If your friends around you love you, they'll wish you the best and want only what's going to make you happy.

> **~ Meagan Good** *(1981)*
> *American actress, author*

➢ Don't let anyone steal ya joy! There's always someone miserable trying to bring you down … you just wish them well and proceed on enjoying your life.

> **~ Missy Elliott** *(1971)*
> *American rapper, singer, songwriter, record*
> *producer, dancer, actress, philanthropist*

➢ Don't wait for the stars to align, reach up and rearrange them the way you want … create your own constellation.

> **~ Pharrell Williams** *(1973)*
> *American singer, rapper, songwriter, record producer, fashion*
> *designer, entrepreneur, formed the record production duo*
> *The Neptunes, producing hip-hop and R&B music*

CHAPTER 5

On Dreaming

What is life without dreaming? Big or small, dreams give us the inner drive to pursue something greater in our lives. Dreams give us the opportunity to think outside the box and envision infinite possibilities for ourselves.

Making your dreams come true is a totally different story. Like lotto, you have to be in it to win it. You have to pursue your dreams ferociously on a daily basis. They should not lie dormant in your mind, heart, and soul, and then die with you. Making them a reality is your assignment in life.

We all have wild dreams, or so they seem. But even the wildest dreams can become a reality if you put in a sincere effort, hard work, and have the willpower to see the vision through to the end. These visions are a part of your reality, and you can make them happen as long as you recognize that they are always within your reach.

Reverend Martin Luther King Jr. is known for his famous 1963 "I Have a Dream" speech. He hoped to capture both the necessity for change and the potential of hope in American society. He had an enormous dream for Negroes (the term used at the time) in America. He urged America to make its promise of democracy a reality by finally freeing all Negroes. Though a hundred years had passed since they were promised freedom in the Emancipation Proclamation of 1863, true freedom had not yet been granted.

The lives of Negroes were still crippled by segregation and discrimination. He believed they were exiled in their own land. He spoke of the Constitution and the Declaration of Independence, which promised that all men would be guaranteed the unalienable rights of life, liberty, and the pursuit of happiness, none of which were honored at the time of his speech.

The civil rights movement of 1954 to 1968—a struggle by African Americans to end legalized racial discrimination, disenfranchisement, and racial segregation in the United States—greatly helped to propel these unalienable rights into fruition. Without Reverend King's clear vision, unwavering fortitude, and "lofty" dream, our ancestors may not have been motivated to band together and fight for their human rights to freedom and equality. Things may not be perfect today, but Reverend King's dream has come true on many fronts.

Dreaming helps to stretch our imaginations into a realm where we can truly see ourselves becoming who we know we are. It expands our minds to envision what we can potentially do. There is no need to doubt yourself or be afraid of dreaming because dreams do come true every day.

My lifelong dream was to become a writer. A legitimate author. At first, I did not believe I was talented or educated enough to pursue this path, but I never stopped writing. I wrote in my journal, I wrote essays, I began—but didn't finish—books. I wrote songs, I wrote poems, I wrote to-do lists. I eventually found an outlet writing and selling greeting cards to Blue Mountain Arts. I seemed to find my niche with this company and eventually not only had cards published but was also published in calendars and anthologies. I was never happier than when this dream of being a published writer came true. I was scared though. I did not venture beyond greeting cards because that was my comfort zone, and I knew I was good at it. I continue to freelance for them.

Although I had been published, something was missing. I did not feel as if my dream was truly fulfilled because my main goal was to write books, magazine articles, and potentially become a columnist. I wanted a full career in writing. Again, I was scared. Scared of what? I'm not quite sure. In the writing game, you get used to rejection, so that wasn't it. I wondered if it could be that I was scared to succeed, but all my thoughts centered on failure. If I actually put in the work and obtained my goal of writing a book, what would I do then? What if no one wanted to publish it? What if it sucked? What if I was a one-hit wonder? There were so many negative what-ifs that my mind raced with doubt after doubt. But my body, mind, and fingers kept trudging on. I was inspired by the words of friends and strangers alike to put my all into making my dream come true.

You are reading the first installment of my dream. It was inspired by the life-altering words of strangers. The dream I was so afraid of has become my reality, and I could not be prouder of my tenacity to see this thing through to the end. Writing is in my blood, and to deny that is to deny who I am at my core. I did not want to doubt myself anymore, and my hard work has led to my dream coming true in real time.

We are what we dream. We can make our dreams a reality. We can find joy in dreaming and watching the finished product of our relentlessness bring our souls alive through a single thought that began in our heads.

Never stop dreaming, and never stop attempting to make those dreams come true. No matter how far-fetched they may seem to you or those around you, know that you have the wherewithal to make it happen for yourself. Rosa Parks did it. Rick Ross did it. Barack Obama did it. Issa Rae did it. Steph Curry did it. My younger brother PJ did it when he became a registered nurse. No one is better than anyone else. We all have dreams that we can make come true, so why don't you begin making your dream happen today? The joy that follows is all-encompassing and will lift your spirit in a way you never knew existed.

Keep dreaming. Just make it your life's goal to make your dreams come true!

On Dreaming

➤ We spend most of our lives cutting down our ambitions because the world has told us to think small. Dreams express what your soul is telling you, so as crazy as your dream might seem – even to you – I don't care: you have to let that out.

~ Eleni Gabre-Madhin
Ethiopian-Swiss economist, former Chief Executive
Officer of the Ethiopia Commodity Exchange

➤ We become what we believe.

~ Oprah Winfrey *(1954)*
Moved to Baltimore from her hometown in Kosciusko, Mississippi
in 1976, where she hosted 'People Are Talking'

➤ No one can negotiate their dreams. Dreams must be free to flee and fly high. No government, no legislature, has a right to limit your dreams. You should never agree to surrender your dreams.

~ Jesse Jackson *(1941)*
American civil rights activist, Baptist minister, politician

➤ I feel that I am a citizen of the American dream and that the revolutionary struggle of which I am a part is a struggle against the American nightmare.

~ Eldridge Cleaver *(1935-1998)*
Became an early leader of the Black Panther Party

➤ Hold fast to dreams, for if dreams die, life is a broken winged bird that cannot fly.

~ Langston Hughes *(1902-1967)*
American poet, social activist, novelist, playwright, columnist

➤ Stay far from timid, only make moves when your heart is in it, and live the phrase the sky's the limit.

~ **Notorious B.I.G.** *(1972-1997)*
American rapper in the New York and Gangsta rap
traditions, who ranks among the greatest rappers ever

➤ Dream! Dream! And then go for it.

~ **Desmond TuTu** *(1931)*
South African Cleric and Theologian

➤ We all have dreams. In order to make dreams come into reality, it takes an awful lot of determination, dedication, self-discipline, and effort.

~ **Jesse Owens** *(1913-1980)*
American track and field athlete

➤ Big dreams turn into big things.

~ **Meek Mill** *(1987)*
American rapper, songwriter, activist

➤ Every great dream begins with a dreamer. Always remember, you have within you the strength, the patience, and the passion to reach for the stars to change the world.

~ **Harriett Tubman** *(died 1913)*
American abolitionist and political activist, born into slavery, she escaped
and made 13 missions to rescue 70 enslaved people using the network of
anti-slavery activists and safe houses known as the Underground Railroad

➤ Hold on to your dreams of a better life and stay committed to striving to realize it.

~ **Earl G. Graves, Sr.** *(1935-2020)*
American entrepreneur, publisher, businessman,
philanthropist, founder of Black Enterprise Magazine

➤ I did it for all the fierce Black women on the front lines of the movement and for all the little Black girls who are watching us. I did it because I am free.

~ **Bree Newsome**
American filmmaker, musician, speaker, activist who drew national attention in 2015 when she climbed the flagpole in front of the South Carolina Capitol building and lowered the Confederate battle flag

➤ Anything is possible. You gotta dream like you never seen obstacles.

~ **J. Cole** *(1985)*
His 2014 release 'Forest Hills Drive' premiered at No. 1 on the Billboard 200, won Billboard's Rap Album of the Year, and was certified double platinum

➤ Your passion is that one thing you can't stop thinking about, that thing you wake up thinking about in the morning, go to sleep thinking about at night, that thing that you would do for free!

~ **Charlamagne Tha God** *(1978)*
A co-host of the nationally syndicated radio show 'The Breakfast Club' with DJ Envy and Angela Yee

➤ Often, people who can do, don't because they're afraid of what people that can't do will say about them doing.

~ **Trevor Noah**
Most successful comedian in Africa, the host of the Emmy and Peabody Award winning 'The Daily Show' on Comedy Central

➤ The best way to make dreams come true is to wake up.

~ **Dr. Mae C. Jemison** *(1956)*
American engineer, physician

➤ Never underestimate the power of dreams and the influence on the human spirit. We are all the same in this notion: the potential for greatness lives within each of us.

~ **Wilma Rudolph** *(1940-1994)*
World-record-holding Olympic champion and international sports icon in track and field following her successes in the 1956 and 1960 Olympic Games

➤ Life without dreaming is life without meaning.

~ **Wale** *(1984)*
Recorded the original music theme for the popular ESPN sports talk show 'First Take'

➤ I motivate others by making sure that they understand to go after their dreams and don't let anyone tell you you can't. If you are motivated enough and put the work in, you can achieve anything in life that you set your mind to.

~ **Magic Johnson** *(1959)*
American retired professional basketball player, former president of basketball operations of the Los Angeles Lakers, prominent HIV/AIDS activist

➤ Don't be afraid to be ambitious about your goals. Hard work never stops. Neither should your dreams.

~ **Dwayne Johnson** *(1972)*
American-Canadian actor, producer, businessman, retired professional wrestler, former American football player, known by his ring name 'The Rock'

➤ I'll be damned if I sit around another year, dreamin' dreams hopin' somehow that they just appear.

~ **J. Cole** *(1985)*
Signed on with Jay-Z's Roc Nation in 2009 and has produced for artists like Kendrick Lamar and Janet Jackson

➢ No matter where you are from, your dreams are valid.

~ Lupida Nyong'o *(1983)*
First Kenyan-Mexican actress to win an Academy Award, author, fashion icon

➢ Be strategic and resilient in the pursuit of your dreams. That sounds like a cheesy quote, right? But nah, I'm serious. Resilience is one hell of a quality to master and not many have the skin for it.

~ Tiffany D. Jackson
American author of young adult fiction, horror filmmaker

➢ Chase your dream, work to the extreme.

~ Tyra Banks *(1973)*
American television personality, producer,
businesswoman, actress, author, model, singer

➢ If your dream ain't bigger than you, there's a problem with your dream.

~ Deion Sanders *(1967)*
American retired professional football and baseball player who
is a sports analyst, he played 14 seasons in the NFL

➢ Action is what separates the do-ers from the dreamers.

~ Lennox Lewis *(1965)*
British retired professional boxer who competed from 1989-2003,
three-time world heavyweight champion, two-time lineal champion,
remains the last heavyweight to hold the undisputed title

➢ Too many of us are not living our dreams because we are living our fears.

~ Les Brown *(1945)*
American motivational speaker, author, radio DJ,
former television host, former politician

➤ I want to be the voice of the people; Black, White, everyday oppressed people. A person trying to make it and to do it right.

~ **Common** *(1972)*
American rapper, actor, writer, won an Oscar for Best Achievement in Music Written for Motion Pictures (Original Song) 'Glory,' with John Legend

➤ No person has the right to rain on your dreams.

~ **Marian Wright Edelman** *(1939)*
American activist for children's rights

➤ They said I would never make it, but I was built to break the mold. The only dream I've been chasing is my own.

~ **Alicia Keys** *(1981)*
A classically trained pianist, she began composing songs by age 12

➤ A star dies in heaven every time you snatch away someone's dream.

~ **Gloria Naylor** *(1950-2016)*
American novelist known for the novel 'The Women of Brewster Place'

➤ Magic lies in changing what seems impossible.

~ **Carol Moseley Braun** *(1947)*
American diplomat, politician, lawyer, the first female African American in the United States Senate from 1993-1999

➤ Black people have always been America's wilderness in search of a promised land.

~ **Cornel West** *(1953)*
American philosopher, political activist, social critic, author, public intellectual, focuses on the role of race, gender, and class in American society

➤ Where there is no vision, there is no hope.

~ **George Washington Carver** *(Died 1943)*
American agricultural scientist, inventor

➢ Within our dreams and aspirations we find our opportunities.

~ Sugar Ray Leonard *(1956)*
American former professional boxer, motivational speaker, actor

➢ Don't downgrade your dream to match your reality. Upgrade your faith to match your destiny.

~ DeVon Franklin *(1978)*
American Hollywood producer, bestselling author,
renowned preacher, motivational speaker

➢ Don't look for your dreams to become true; look to become true to your dreams.

~ Michael Bernard Beckwith *(1956)*
American New Thought minister, author and Founder of the
Agape International Spiritual Center in Beverly Hills, CA

CHAPTER 6

On Being Inspired

Inspiration can be found anywhere you are, from anything you see or hear: an aria at the opera, a mother breastfeeding her baby, a minister's message that speaks directly to you, a song's lyrics, a pair of pants finally fitting, or a random act of kindness.

To be inspired is to be alive. To live an inspired life is to be grateful for each and every moment that you breathe air into your lungs and have the freedom to live life with no boundaries and no regrets.

There are no limitations on inspiration, and that is what's so exciting about it. It is everywhere and in everything. You just have to recognize it and take in the refreshing thoughts it opens your mind to. Revel in it and see all the emotion it brings to your everyday life.

Live in the moment. Let the moment engulf you and hold you hostage in its light. Do not think about yesterday or tomorrow; stay in the here and now. Allow that moment to inspire you to live your best life right in that moment. Do not get distracted by what is happening around you. Stay inspired in the joy of the moment, and you will thrive.

A moment of inspiration leads to a lifetime of hope. Be inspired in your life, and you will soon see the sunshine through the rain. All of a sudden you will notice the good even in the bad, and your perspective will shift to a higher vibration.

Inspiration is defined as the process of being mentally stimulated to do or feel something, especially to do something creative. Strive for inspiration even in the smallest details of your life. Look for inspiration as you move through your day. Seek it. Find positive sources of inspiration and allow yourself to grab hold of these sometimes-tiny morsels of encouragement. This will both uplift you and make you see that life is not so bad after all.

What inspires me may not inspire you. There is nothing wrong with that. We are all different and comprehend and value things in different ways. The goal here is to find what *your* inspiration is and allow your spirit to guide you in that direction. Allow your heart to soak in all the good that comes from it. Allow your mind to savor that joy.

Quotes derived from the urban poetry that is called hip-hop music and their artists are included in this book not only because they deserve to be but because they inspire me greatly. I write to it. I jam to it. I rap with it. I admire it. I am in awe of its ingenuity.

It is so inspiring that our strong African American men, as boys, created a whole new genre of music that has crossed over from the neighborhoods and street corners to *Billboard*'s top 100 and the Grammy awards, from the Songwriters Hall of Fame to the Pulitzer Prize in music. Hip-hop has finally received the institutional legitimacy that it deserves. I am beyond proud to be a part of the culture from which hip-hop arose. It proves to me that we, as a people, are fierce and can turn anything into something special if we are inspired to do so. As Nas says, "Turnin' nothin' into somthin' is God work, and you get nothin' without struggle and hard work."

The quotes in this chapter have such diverse points of view, and I love this chapter for that reason. We all receive inspiration differently for a variety of reasons. You may not understand one person's source of inspiration, but that is not for you to figure out. Discover and define your own sources of inspiration and allow it to change your viewpoint and your life. Strive to be inspired every day!

On Being Inspired

➢ God may allow us at times to hit rock bottom to show us He's the rock-at-the-bottom.

~ Kirk Franklin *(1970)*
American gospel musician, songwriter, choir director, author

➢ Just sitting in silence is one of the best things a man can do.

~ Nas *(1973)*
Released twelve studio albums since 1994, with seven of them certified platinum and multi-platinum in the U.S.

➢ I don't want a Black History month. Black History is American History.

~ Morgan Freeman *(1937)*
American actor, director, narrator, the recipient of an Academy Award, Golden Globe Award, and a Screen Actors Guild Award

➢ I see your life as already artful, just waiting, and ready for you to make it art.

~ Toni Morrison *(1931)*
American novelist, essayist, editor, teacher

➢ We are imperfect creatures, but we should start reaching for the better you, the better me.

~ Sidney Poitier *(1927)*
Bahamian-American film director, author, diplomat

➢ The moment you give up, is the moment you let someone else win.

~ Kobe Bryant *(1978-2020)*
As a shooting guard, he entered the NBA directly from high school

➤ I believe everyone in the world is born with genius-level talent. Apply yourself to whatever you're genius at, and you can do anything in the world.

~ **Jay-Z** *(1969)*
Founded Roc Nation in 2008, which is a full-service entertainment
company that houses a record label, a talent agency for clients, philanthropy,
a school, apparel, touring, and a concerts production company

➤ Strong convictions are the secret of surviving deprivation; your spirit can be full even when your stomach is empty.

~ **Nelson Mandela** *(1918-2013)*
South Africa's first Black head of state and the first elected
in a fully representative democratic election

➤ I'm for human lib, the liberation of all people, not just Black people or female people or gay people.

~ **Richard Pryor** *(1940-2005)*
American stand-up comedian, actor, writer, widely regarded as one of
the greatest and most influential stand-up comedians of all time

➤ You start to live when a moment feels like a lifetime.

~ **Chris Brown** *(1989)*
American singer, songwriter, dancer, actor

➤ If I have done anything in life worth attention, I feel sure that I inherited the disposition from my mother.

~ **Booker T. Washington** *(1856-1915)*
Between 1890 and 1915, he was the dominant leader in the African
American community and of the contemporary Black elite

➤ The message I'm sending to myself – I can't change the world until I change myself first.

~ **Kendrick Lamar** *(1987)*
His release 'Damn' was the first non-classical or non-jazz recording to
win the Pulitzer Prize for Music and the first for the world of hip-hop

➤ You don't have to be one of those people that accepts things as they are. Every day take responsibility for changing them right where you are.

~ **Cory Booker** *(1969)*
First African American United States Senator from New Jersey (2013-present)

➤ You never know how or when you'll have an impact, or how important your example can be to someone else.

~ **Denzel Washington** *(1954)*
American actor, director, producer, won 2 Golden Globes,
1 Tony Award and 3 Academy Awards

➤ I believe in God, who made of one blood all nations that on earth do dwell. I believe that all men, Black and Brown and White, are brothers, varying through time and opportunity, in form and gift and feature, but differing in no essential particular, and alike in soul and the possibility of infinite development.

~ **W.E.B. Du Bois** *(1868-1963)*
American sociologist, socialist, historian, civil rights
activist, Pan-Africanist, author, writer, editor

➤ Knowledge speaks, but wisdom listens.

~ **Jimi Hendrix** *(1942-1970)*
American rock guitarist, singer, songwriter, widely regarded
as one of the most influential guitarists in history, one of
the most celebrated musicians of the 20th century

➤ I guarantee that the seed you plant in love, no matter how small, will grow into a mighty tree of refuge. We all want a future for ourselves and we must now care enough to create, nurture, and secure a future for our children.

~ **Afeni Shakur** *(1947-2016)*
American activist and businesswoman who was the
mother of the late rapper Tupac Shakur

➢ Greatness occurs when your children love you, when your critics respect you and when you have peace of mind.

~ Quincy Jones *(1933)*
American record producer, multi-instrumentalist, songwriter, composer, arranger, film and television producer, won 28 Grammys and the Grammy Legend Award in 1992

➢ Working with these kids today and being able to just help them set goals for themselves and work with them towards their goals is a great thing. I think sometimes it's better than breaking the color barrier.

~ Willie O'Ree *(1935)*
Canadian former professional ice hockey player, known best for being the first Black player in the National Hockey League as a winger for the Boston Bruins

➢ Race means family and all Black people, whether they like it or not, are family.

~ Kola Boof *(1969)*
Sudanese-American novelist

➢ I am where I am because I believe in all possibilities.

~ Whoopi Goldberg *(1955)*
One of sixteen entertainers to have won an Emmy Award, a Grammy Award, an Academy Award, and a Tony Award

➢ So I just had to step up how I was doing it and the moment that I stepped up and the moment I focused all my energy on that is when things started to happen. So there's a direct relationship between my inspiration and my output.

~ Talib Kweli *(1975)*
American rapper, entrepreneur, activist

➤ Hip-hop isn't just music. It is also a spiritual movement of the Blacks! You can't just call hip-hop a trend!

~ Lauryn Hill *(1975)*
Often regarded as one of the greatest rappers of all time,
as well as being a pioneer in the Neo soul genre

➤ Smiling is the best way to face every problem, to crush every fear and to hide every pain.

~ Will Smith *(1968)*
American actor, rapper, in 2007, Newsweek called him
"The most powerful actor in Hollywood"

➤ I decided Blacks should not have to experience the difficulties I had faced, so I decided to open a flying school and teach other Black women to fly.

~ Bessie Coleman *(1892-1926)*
American civil aviator, the first woman of African-American descent,
and also the first of Native American descent, to hold a pilot license

➤ It is our duty to fight for our freedom. It is our duty to win. We must love each other and support each other. We have nothing to lose but our chains.

~ Assata Shakur *(1947)*
American former member of the Black Liberation Army

➤ The best way to fight an alien and oppressive culture is to embrace your own.

~ Afrikan Proverb
Proverb: A short pithy saying in general use,
stating a general truth or piece of advice

➢ The higher purpose of my life is not the song and dance or the acclaim, but to rise up, to pull up others and leave the world and industry a better place.

~ **Viola Davis** *(1965)*
American actress, producer; having won an Academy Award,
an Emmy Award, and two Tony Awards, she is the first
Black thespian to achieve the Triple Crown of Acting

➢ I want to be remembered as someone who used herself and anything she could touch to work for justice and freedom ... I want to be remembered as one who tried.

~ **Dorothy Height** *(1912-2010)*
American civil rights activist, women's rights activist who
specifically focused on African American women, President of
the National Council of Negro Women for forty years

➢ Don't settle for average. Bring your best to the moment. Then, whether it fails or succeeds, at least you know you gave all you had. We need to live the best that's in us.

~ **Angela Bassett** *(1958)*
American actress, director, producer, activist, known for
her biographical film roles, most notably as Tina Turner
in the biopic 'What's Love Got to Do with It'

➢ I always believed that when you follow your heart or your gut, when you really follow the things that feel great to you, you can never lose, because settling is the worst feeling in the world.

~ **Rihanna** *(1988)*
Barbadian singer, songwriter, actress, businesswoman

➢ What you know today can affect what you do tomorrow. But what you know today cannot affect what you did yesterday.

~ **Condolezza Rice** *(1954)*
American political scientist, diplomat, civil servant, professor, served
as the 66th United States Secretary of State from 2005-2009

➢ Sometimes it's the journey that teaches you a lot about your destination.

~ **Drake** *(1986)*
Canadian rapper, singer, songwriter, actor, businessman

➢ At this moment, the Negroes must begin to do the very thing which they have been taught they cannot do.

~ **Carter Woodson** *(1875-1950)*
American historian, author, journalist

➢ Emancipate yourself from mental slavery, none but ourselves can free our mind.

~ **Bob Marley** *(1945-1981)*
Considered one of the pioneers of Reggae

➢ Somebody has to stand when other people are sitting. Somebody has to speak when other people are quiet.

~ **Bryan Stevenson** *(1959)*
American lawyer, social justice advocate, founder/
executive director of the Equal Justice Initiative

CHAPTER 7

On Self-Worth

If you do not believe in yourself, who will? What you believe about yourself appears in your life in unbelievable ways. Unless you are extremely self-aware, you may have no idea how you present yourself to the world. Do you value yourself? Are you confident? Are you self-conscious? Do you like yourself? Are you insecure? Are you a bully? What does your self-worth express about you in the real world?

Your self-worth can determine how you present yourself to society. It can define how you move, what you tolerate, and how you react to a variety of situations. It creates a ripple effect in many areas of your life. Self-worth and self-esteem work hand in hand with the way you feel about yourself and how you react to feelings of self-love or self-loathing.

Some African Americans have a hard time deciphering their worth in this world. Our ancestors were stolen, shackled, and forced into slavery. They were considered less than animals. They were isolated from their families, raped, and treated as though they were not worth anything. They were lynched and dragged to their deaths. They were given no rights, no individuality, and no freedom. How was positive self-worth supposed to form under those circumstances?

Through strength and resilience, they survived the daily beatings of their bodies and their minds, but their souls had to be broken. As a community they had to build each other up while simultaneously being broken down. Can you imagine trying to believe in yourself while being treated like you were no one to be believed in? It must have taken decades to build up their self-esteem and sense of self-worth because of the circumstances they had lived under for centuries. Self-determination and courage had to be part of what helped them to rebuild their sense of self.

Sadly, in 2020 the climate of racial inequality continues and has been greatly exacerbated, blatantly showing us that Black lives do not seem to matter whatsoever. With the frequency and pervasiveness of police brutality against innocent Black and Brown people not being addressed, along with a standing president who wears his racism on his sleeve and does not intervene to restore a sense of peace and solidarity, our self-worth is being further damaged by the systemic racism that persists endlessly in our infrastructure. The public outcry for change has long been ignored and has caused an uproar in communities across the United States. The heavily attended protests that we see daily in cities not only across the nation but throughout the world are active cries for the unheard to be heard once and for all. Americans are tired of the social injustices that continue to oppress our communities with nothing being done to correct them. Change must come sooner rather than later. Otherwise, I believe, this world will implode, and a race war will ensue.

Given our history, believing in ourselves and our worth is an incredible gift that not all of us have received organically. African American slaves certainly did not receive that gift. Modern-day African Americans are not receiving that gift. We have to work at building up that belief within ourselves with education, prayer, meditation, self-love, and simply realizing that we are enough just as we are, regardless of how society treats us.

You have to wake up every day and know that you are the bomb. Know that you are beautiful, kind, smart, wise, important, and your own wonderful and unique self. Sure, we all have qualities to work on, but that should not interfere with our innate sense of pride about ourselves. Enhance yourself in whatever way you see fit, but do it for yourself. Do it because you want to keep improving yourself. Do it despite what society is showing us. Rather, do it because you know that you are worthy of betterment. Do not do it out of peer pressure, to get a partner, or because you think that your self-esteem will grow if other people notice you. None of those opinions matter. Only your opinion matters.

A sense of self-worth radiates from within. It may have been instilled in you as a young child, or you may have identified your own wonderfulness and run with it. Either way, it is essential that you believe in yourself and your abilities. You are the only you on this earth, and you are a mighty fine prize. Remember that.

Positive self-worth is a prerequisite to inner peace and happiness. It is a quality that you owe to yourself, for yourself, by yourself. Do not look outward to try to gain this sense of self. Always look inward and exude who you know to be to the world. You are an amazing human just the way you are. Now believe that in your heart and soul, and project it on a daily basis!

On Self-Worth

➤ There was a time when I didn't like myself at all. I thought I was a cruel joke. But now I've come to realize that maybe I'm not cute, but I am beautiful.

*~ **Cee Lo Green** (1975)*
American singer, rapper, composer, record producer, actor

➤ Your self-worth is determined by you. You don't have to depend on someone telling you who you are.

*~ **Beyonce Knowles** (1981)*
Multi-platinum, Grammy Award winning recording artist who's
acclaimed for her thrilling vocals, videos, and live shows

➤ Whatever we believe about ourselves and our ability comes true for us.

*~ **Susan L. Taylor** (1946)*
American journalist, editor, writer

➤ Waking up in truth is so much better than living in a lie.

*~ **Idris Elba** (1972)*
Was appointed Officer of the Order of the British Empire (OBE) by Queen
Elizabeth II in the 2016 New Years Honours for his services in drama

➤ Self-esteem means knowing you are the dream.

*~ **Oprah Winfrey** (1954)*
In 1971, she entered Tennessee State University and began
working in television broadcasting in Nashville

➤ You are your best thing.

*~ **Toni Morrison** (1931)*
Won the Pulitzer Prize and American Book Award in 1988 for
"Beloved," awarded the Nobel Prize in Literature in 1993

➤ Accept and acknowledge your own brilliance. Stop waiting for others to tell you how great you are! Believe it for yourself and about yourself.

*~ **Iyanla Vanzant** (1953)*
American inspirational speaker, New Thought spiritual teacher

➤ If you have no confidence in self, you are twice defeated in the race of life.

*~ **Marcus Garvey** (1887-1940)*
A proponent of the Black Nationalism and Pan-Africanism movements,
inspiring the Nation of Islam and the Rastafarian movement

➤ Each individual has got to look themselves in the mirror and try and see what they can do better. Period. Point blank.

*~ **Jason Kidd** (1973)*
American professional basketball coach, former NBA player who
is currently an assistant coach for the Los Angeles Lakers

➤ Seek the truth. Tell the truth. Live in the truth.

*~ **Isaiah Washington** (1963)*
American actor, producer, internet personality,
best known for 'Grey's Anatomy'

➤ When you get to know yourself, you get to know everyone and everything on the planet.

*~ **Rakim** (1968)*
Widely regarded as one of the most influential and most skilled MC's of all time

➤ I am a feminist, and what that means to me is much the same as the meaning of the fact that I am Black; it means that I must undertake to love myself and to respect myself as though my very life depends upon self-love and self-respect.

*~ **June Jordan** (1936-2002)*
Jamaican-American self-identified bisexual, poet, essayist, teacher, activist

➢ A man without knowledge of himself and his heritage is like a tree without roots.

~ **Dick Gregory** *(1932-2017)*
American comedian, civil right activist, conspiracy
theorist, social critic, writer, actor

➢ The battles that count aren't the ones for gold medals. The struggles within yourself – the invisible, inevitable battles inside all of us – that's where it's at.

~ **Jesse Owens** *(1913-1980)*
Four-time gold medalist in the 1936 Olympics in track and field

➢ As long as we are not ourselves, we will try to be what other people are.

~ **Malidoma Patrice Some** *(1956)*
West African writer and workshop leader primarily in the field of spirituality

➢ What you're thinking is what you're becoming.

~ **Muhammad Ali** *(1942-2016)*
Nicknamed 'The Greatest,' one of the greatest boxers of all time

➢ We're our own worst enemy. You doubt yourself more than anybody else ever will. If you can get past that, you can be successful.

~ **Michael Strahan** *(1971)*
American television host, former professional football player who
played his entire 15-year career with the New York Giants

➢ You can be the lead in your own life.

~ **Kerry Washington** (1977)
American actress, producer, director, known for her role
as Olivia Pope in the ABC series 'Scandal'

➢ I didn't want to have to deal with having any moniker or separation between the self that I see and know myself as.

~ **Mos Def** *(1973)*
American rapper, singer, actor, activist

➢ I am not my hair, I am not this skin, I am the soul that lives within.

~ **India Arie** *(1975)*
American singer, songwriter

➢ I'm convinced that we Black women possess a special indestructible strength that allows us to not only get down, but to get up, get through and get over.

~ **Janet Jackson** *(1966)*
American singer, songwriter, actress, dancer

➢ Deal with yourself as an individual worthy of respect and make everyone else deal with you the same way.

~ **Nikki Giovanni** *(1943)*
Her poems helped to define the African American
voice of the 1960's, 70's and beyond

➢ "I can't" are two words that have never been in my vocabulary. I believe in me more than anything in this world.

~ **Wilma Rudolph** *(1940-1994)*
In 1960, she became the first American woman to win three
gold medals in track and field in a single Olympics

➢ Low self-esteem in Black children is a direct result of what they have not been taught about who they were. Although knowledge of self is essential to academic progress, race pride is even more essential than knowledge of self.

~ **Dr. Umar Johnson**
American world-renowned speaker, author, certified school psychologist,
activist aiming to improve his community, Dr. of Clinical Psychology

➢ Trust yourself. Think for yourself. Speak for yourself. Be yourself. Imitation is suicide.

~ **Marva Collins** *(1936-2015)*
American educator

➢ Always be yourself. At the end of the day, that's all you've really got; when you strip everything down, that's all you've got, so always be yourself.

~ **Al Roker** *(1954)*
American weather forecaster, journalist, television personality, actor, author, the current weather anchor on NBC's Today Show

➢ If you cannot find peace within yourself, you will never find it anywhere else.

~ **Marvin Gaye** *(1939-1984)*
American singer, songwriter, record producer, helped to shape the sound of Motown in the 1960's

➢ 100 is worth 100 no matter how dirty or crumbled it may be. Similarly, you don't lose your worth because you've been through something.

~ **Reverend Run**
A practicing minister

➢ I'm not interested in trying to work on people's perceptions. I am who I am, and if you don't take the time to learn about that, then your perception is going to be your problem.

~ **Jim Brown** *(1936)*
American retired professional football player, sports analyst, actor

➢ Be who you are and let everyone love that person.

~ **Wiz Khalifa** *(1987)*
American rapper, singer, songwriter, actor

➤ You don't have to be anything but yourself to be worthy.

~ Tarana Burke *(1973)*
American civil rights activist who founded the Me Too Movement in 2006
to raise awareness of the pervasiveness of sexual abuse and assault in society

➤ You don't have to become something you're not to be better than you were.

~ Sidney Poitier *(1927)*
In 1964, became the first Bahamian and Black actor to win an Academy
Award and a Golden Globe for best actor for 'Lilies of the Field'

➤ Not only is your story worth telling, but it can be told in words so painstakingly eloquent that it becomes a song.

~ Gloria Naylor *(1950-2016)*
Spent seven years as a Jehovah's Witness missionary

➤ I don't want to be a supermodel. I want to be a role model.

~ Queen Latifah *(1970)*
American rapper, singer, songwriter, actress, producer

➤ Lack of confidence is what makes you want to change somebody else's mind. When you're OK, you don't need to convince anyone else in order to empower yourself.

~ Jada Pinkett Smith *(1971)*
American actress, singer, songwriter, screenwriter, businesswoman

➤ When you take care of yourself, you're a better person for others. When you feel good about yourself, you treat others better.

~ Solange Knowles *(1986)*
American singer, songwriter, record producer, performance artist, actress

➤ If you prioritize yourself, you are going to save yourself.

~ Gabrielle Union *(1972)*
American actress, voice artist, activist, author

➤ If we gave our children sound self-love, they will be able to deal with whatever life puts before them.

~ Bell Hooks *(1952)*
American author, professor, feminist, social activist

➤ I'd rather be hated for what I am than to be loved for what I'm not.

~ Chuck D *(1960)*
As the leader of the rap group Public Enemy, he helped to create politically and socially conscious hip-hop music in the mid-1980's with co-founder Flavor Flav

➤ You are no better than anyone else, and no one is better than you.

~ Katherine Johnson *(1918-2020)*
American mathematician whose calculations of orbital mechanics as a NASA employee were critical to the success of the first and subsequent U.S. crewed spaceflights

CHAPTER 8

On Power and Fear

African Americans in the United States have a pervasive history of powerlessness and fear. We were powerless when we were herded like animals and brought to this country from our native land and forced into slavery. We were fearful when we were set free and routinely hunted, lynched, and killed because a portion of the country did not agree with Abraham Lincoln's Emancipation Proclamation. The powerlessness and fear has waned, but it still exists within our African American community.

As the country slowly grew and evolved, people of color made great strides in securing a piece of the pie. But much still needs to be changed before we are truly considered equals. It is my fear that this will not happen in my lifetime.

The British historian Lord Acton wrote, "Power corrupts, and absolute power corrupts absolutely." The absolute power and control that the White community has had over African Americans for centuries continues to this day. Sure, there has been much reform, but much substantive change is still required in order for our community to feel and be treated as equal.

While Barack Obama made history when, in 2009, he was inaugurated as the first African American president, to me, the racial divide seemed to form a wider chasm during his presidency. Racism is not dead is what I learned from watching his journey unfold. Racism seemed to gain even more momentum in 2017, when Donald Trump took office. Many of his supporters clearly wear their racism on their sleeves, and all the social progress Mr. Obama made seemed pointless.

My position is the fact that a Black man was the most powerful person in the country, much of White America felt a sense of fear and powerlessness for the first time in their history. President Obama did not abuse his power, so there was no need for this fear. Yet it existed, nonetheless. I believe that President Obama's ultimate power as commander in chief created fear within much of the faction of the country who were used to having all the power. To have a Black man take over that power for the first time was sobering and frightening to them, and many could not handle it.

I believe that having power can elicit a sense of superiority and entitlement that, after being powerless for so long, the average African American cannot fully identify with. I know I cannot. I have been in positions of power, yet I did not feel superior to those below me. What I did feel was a sense of empowerment and accomplishment. I was proud of myself for achieving such a prominent status. And then fear set in. The fear that this "young, hot, Black chick"—as I was called to my face by my male superior—would not be successful in my new role, which was his prediction. I am proud to say that he was dead wrong. This is the irony of being Black in America. When given the opportunity to excel, the fear of failure often overcomes us and makes us doubt our qualifications when we are more than qualified for our new roles.

It is time we take our power back and leave the fear behind us. All men *were* created equal, whether we are treated that way or not. It is up to each of us to demand equality in our everyday lives. We need to walk with our heads held high, put forth our best qualities, and prove to society—and ourselves—that our powerlessness and fear are behind us. We should look to those positive African American men and women in our lives and in the world as the compasses for our own future accomplishments and successes.

Fear is both a noun and a verb. Use it as a verb. Put action to the fear, and fight through the racism that holds us back from being powerful in our own rights. It is within our power to embrace our power. We should own it and use it to our advantage every moment of our lives. Don't be afraid of power, especially your own. Our personal power helps to propel us forward to achieving our goals and becoming the best versions of ourselves.

The African American community is a powerful force in this world. We must not forget that. We cannot continue to be enslaved within our minds. We must break free from whatever chains bind us and claim our rightful places in this America we call home.

On Power and Fear

➤ Ever since 401 years ago the reason we could never be who we wanted and dreamed to be is because you kept your knee on our neck.

~ Al Sharpton *(1954)*
American civil rights activist, Baptist minister, talk show host, politician

➤ Power's not given to you. You have to take it.

~ Beyonce Knowles *(1981)*
Made her acting debut in 2001 with a starring role in 'Carmen: A Hip Hopera'

➤ You can't separate peace from freedom because no one can be at peace unless he has freedom.

~ Malcolm X *(1925-1965)*
Best known for his time spent as a vocal spokesman for the Nation of Islam

➤ You have to keep your vision clear, cause only a coward lives in fear.

~ Nas *(1973)*
Became a dominant voice in 1990's East Coast hip-hop

➤ I think every individual has his or her own power, and it's a matter of working, taking time and defining what that power is.

~ Jill Scott *(1972)*
American singer, songwriter, model, poet, actress

➤ The most fundamental truth to be told in any art form, as far as Blacks are concerned, is that America is killing us.

~ Sonia Sanchez *(1934)*
American poet, writer, professor, a leading figure in the Black Arts Movement

fear more times myself than I can remember, but I hid it
d a mask of boldness. The brave man is not he who does not
feel afraid, but he who conquers that fear.

~ **Nelson Mandela** *(1918-2013)*
Joined the African National Congress in 1944 when he
helped to form the ANC Youth League (ANCYL)

➢ The most common way people give up their power is by thinking
they don't have any.

~ **Alice Walker** *(1944)*
The first African American woman to win the Pulitzer Prize for Fiction

➢ Money and power don't change you they just further expose your
true self.

~ **Jay-Z** *(1969)*
His name was simultaneously an homage to Jaz-O, who served as a
kind of mentor, and a play on his childhood nickname of "Jazzy," as
well as a reference to the J/Z subway station near his Brooklyn home

➢ I am lucky that whatever fear I have inside me, my desire to win is
always stronger.

~ **Serena Williams** *(1981)*
American professional tennis player, won 23 Grand Slam singles
titles, the most by any man or woman in the open era

➢ There really can be no peace without justice. There can be no
justice without truth. And there can be no truth unless someone
rises up to tell you the truth.

~ **Louis Farrakhan** *(1933)*
American minister, political activist, the leader of the Nation of Islam

➢ I aim for stuff so big, that the dream is bigger than the fear.

~ **Steve Harvey** *(1957)*
American comedian, businessman, entertainer, author

➤ There is no justice in America, but it is the fight for justice that sustains you.

~ **Amari Baracka** *(1934-2014)*
American writer of poetry, drama, fiction, essays, music criticism

➤ Character is power.

~ **Booker T. Washington** *(1856-1915)*
Presidential Advisor to multiple Presidents

➤ I think right about now we have to beware of marketed Malcolms and Martins. Real people do real things.

~ **Chuck D** *(1960)*
One of the most colossal figures in the history of hip-hop and its most respected intellectual

➤ Many and most moments go by with us hardly aware of their passage. But love and hate and fear cause time to snag you, to drag you down like a spider's web holding fast to a doomed fly's wings.

~ **Walter Mosley** *(1952)*
American novelist

➤ Truth is powerful and it prevails.

~ **Sojourner Truth** *(1797-1883)*
American abolitionist, women's rights activist

➤ Fear nothing. Do what you want to do but be educated and intelligent and confident about it.

~ **Idris Elba** *(1972)*
Best known for his work on the television series 'The Wire' and 'Luther'

➢ Black Power is giving power to people who have not had power to determine their destiny.

~ Huey Newton *(1942-1989)*
Revolutionary African American political activist, co-founded the Black Panther Party in 1966

➢ It is not an easy journey, to get to a place where you forgive people. But it is such a powerful place because it frees you.

~ Tyler Perry *(1969)*
In 2019, he announced the opening of the $250 million Tyler Perry Studios in Atlanta, Georgia

➢ I have learned over the years that when one's mind is made up, this diminishes fear; knowing what must be done does away with fear.

~ Rosa Parks *(1913-2005)*
American activist in the civil rights movement, best known for her pivotal role in the Montgomery bus boycott

➢ The clock has been turned back on racial progress in America, though scarcely anyone seems to notice. All eyes are fixed on people like Barack Obama and Oprah Winfrey who have defied the odds and achieved great power, wealth, and fame.

~ Michelle Alexander *(1967)*
American writer, civil rights advocate, opinion columnist for The New York Times, visiting professor at Union Theological Seminary, best known for her 2010 book 'The New Jim Crow: Mass Incarceration in the Age of Colorblindness'

➢ The greatest sin is fear and giving up.

~ Nas *(1973)*
His 1996 release 'It Was Written' debuted at No. 1 on both the pop and R&B charts and went double platinum

➤ Truth is the ultimate power. When the truth comes around, all the lies have to run and hide.

~ Ice Cube *(1969)*
American rapper, actor, producer, director, writer

➤ The secret of life is to have no fear; it's the only way to function.

~ Stokely Carmichael *(1941-1998)*
Prominent Caribbean-American organizer in the civil rights movement in the U.S. and the global Pan-African movement, political activist

➤ You are not that necessary, privileged, or famous. Don't think you're better than someone based on your accumulated things, position, or status.

~ John W. Gray III *(1973)*
American Senior Pastor of Relentless Church in Greenville, SC who continues to serve as an Associate Pastor of America's largest single venue church, Lakewood Church in Houston, TX, author

➤ You ultimately judge the civility of a society not by how it treats the rich, the powerful, the protected and the highly esteemed, but by how it treats the poor, the disfavored and the disadvantaged.

~ Bryan Stevenson *(1959)*
Clinical professor at New York University School of Law

➤ They should know that the law protects them just as it protects everyone else.

~ Maya Wiley
American civil rights activist

➤ My thing is that I don't give no person that much power over my path that I'm walking. Not one person can make or break what I'm doing, except me or God.

~ Nipsey Hussle *(1985-2019)*
American rapper, activist, entrepreneur

➢ If you cannot hear the sound of the genuine in you, you will all of your life spend your days on the ends of strings that somebody else pulls.

~ Howard Thurman *(1899-1981)*
American author, philosopher, theologian, educator,
civil rights leader, prominent religious figure

➢ This is not a Black and White issue. This is a national crisis. I believe this is a crisis ... it's about police officers abusing their power.

~ Erica Garner *(1990-2017)*
American activist who advocated for police reform, became involved in activism following the 2014 death of her father, Eric Garner, after a New York City police officer placed him in a chokehold during an arrest

➢ We have defeated Jim Crow, but now we have to deal with his son, James Crow, Jr. Esquire.

~ Al Sharpton *(1954)*
Outspoken and sometimes controversial political activist, working to lead the fight against racial prejudice and injustice

➢ Every African American I know has two faces. There's the face that we have for ourselves and the face we put on for White America for the places we have to get to.

~ Lee Daniels *(1959)*
American film and television writer, director, producer

➢ The best way to protect young Black, Brown, men of color, women of color, is to actually stop profiling, stop the prejudice, and stop the judgement first.

~ Hill Harper *(1966)*
American actor, author

➢ It's nice to be important, but it's more important to be nice.

~ Reverend Run *(1964)*
Shows his deep spiritual side by posting "Rev's Words of Wisdom" daily on his website

➤ Black people, we are fully deserving of the room and space to fully express our humanity. This is what Black Lives Matter is truly about.

~ Opal Tometi *(1984)*
Nigerian-American human rights activist, writer,
strategist, community organizer

CHAPTER 9

On Loving

It has been said that love costs all that we are and all that we will ever be. That is a daunting statement, but it does not have to be a daunting circumstance. Love is all around us. It is far more than relational love; that's the cherry. It is the sun, the moon, and the stars. It is our parents and our ancestors. It is a child's laughter. It is the music of Bob Marley and Phoebe Snow. It is good health and a strong spirit. It is you, and it is me. Life is nothing without love.

Often when we think of love, we think of it solely in a relationship scenario. Of course we would all like to love and be loved. We would like to find our life partners and spend the rest of our lives together in bliss. It just isn't that easy, is it? No, but it is possible every day.

Romantic love is a complex entity that can elude and mystify us all. It can conjure up strong affection, emptiness, white-hot passion, insecurity, oneness, and a host of other complicated emotions. It often seems uncontrollable, ergo, "*falling* in love." Other times love comes alive slowly through friendship, trials and tribulations, loss, longing, and always, always with a whole lot of work. True, soul-shattering love is never easy, but it is always worth the effort.

No one should expect loving to be the same for everyone. Love resides within our souls, and there is no guarantee how it is going to show up in the world, who or what is going to be the recipient of that love, or how long it will last. Romantic or otherwise, love is a blessing that all of us should be grateful to experience. Love breathes life into our bodies and awakens emotions we may not have known existed.

I have been fortunate to experience many forms of love in my life, none sweeter than the next. The love for my nieces, nephew, great-niece, and great-nephews rates right up there with experiencing love with whom I thought was my soul mate. My love for macaroni and cheese is on par with the love I have for music. My love for Converse shoes likens to my love for my best friends. My love for fresh air does not overshadow the great love I have for my deceased mother. It is all love, one no more passionate than the next. All have spaces in my heart that are not in competition with another. There is a place in my heart for all the love I am lucky enough to be blessed with.

The strength of Black love is real. I believe that love between a Black man and a Black woman is on another level that is destined. We have gone through so much oppression as a people that when two like-minded Black people fall in love, it is often a ride-or-die situation. It is unbreakable under the right conditions. Our history of slavery, injustice, and inequality forms a special bond that other races may not be able to identify with in quite the same manner or with the same verve.

My belief in Black love does not dim the light of love discovered by those between different races or those of the same sex. Like any love relationship, interracial and same-sex love can be magical and can open people's lives to the intricacies of their respective worlds.

An interracial union can bring understanding to the different races and elicit hope, learning, and acceptance of the differences and similarities between the two. By embracing the history of the other, a deeper level of connection can be reached, and love will be free to blossom like wildflowers.

I believe that you are born with a predisposition to one sex or another. I do not believe that a same-sex union is always a choice. I believe that homosexuality is a natural progression of one's inner truth, and to deny that truth is to live a life that is not authentic. With understanding and acceptance, same-sex unions are as natural as any other union and will flourish in love's light.

Love is where you find it. If you are fortunate to find it in any form, I say welcome it with open arms. As long as you love yourself first and love each other fully, all love can conquer any obstacle and overcome the challenges life will set before it.

We are finally starting to see positive portrayals of Black love on television and in movies. Realistic stories reflecting real-life situations. The truth of life as Black people, couples, and families are actually in rotation for the rest of the world to see. It must be mind-blowing for other races to see that our normalcy is not unlike theirs. This is relatively new to the screen, and it is quite refreshing.

This phenomenon has come about mostly due to our talented African American writers, producers, and directors such as Tyler Perry, Lena Waithe, Ava Duvernay, Issa Rae, Regina King, Mara Brock Akil, Kasi Lemmons, and Jordan Peele. Newcomers and legends alike are taking it upon themselves to make their own ways in Hollywood, portraying our lives as they are—normal. We are not caricatures; rather, we are interesting and real. I am proud that these modern-day pioneers and visionaries are taking the world by storm and making quality, thought-provoking stories on Black life and Black love. It has been a long time in the making.

John Legend said, "Love is the end and the beginning. Even when you lose, you're winning." You can never give enough love or receive enough love. The wise person gives far more love than he or she is looking to receive because you get what you give in this life. Karma is real and working for or against you every day. Please allow it to work *for* you.

Think of love as the light that leads your way, as the rainbow across the valley and the cool breeze on a hot summer day. Remember love as a precious blessing that you deserve to have every day and in every way. There is no life without love. Be love, and you will be given life.

On Loving

> Love takes off masks that we fear we cannot live without and know we cannot live within.

~ **James Baldwin** *(1924-1987)*
His essays, as collected in 'Notes of a Native Son,' explore the
intricacies of racial, sexual, and class distinctions in Western society,
most notably with regard to the mid-twentieth-century United States

> You've got to learn to leave the table when love's no longer being served.

~ **Nina Simone** *(1933-2003)*
American singer, songwriter, musician, arranger, civil rights activist

> Love is unconditional; love liberates; love is the reason why I do what I do, and so I think it is the greatest gift we have.

~ **BeBe Winans** *(1962)*
American gospel and R&B singer, a member of the
Winans family, most of whom are gospel singers

> Even if it makes others uncomfortable, I will love who I am.

~ **Janelle Monae** *(1985)*
American singer, songwriter, rapper, actress, producer

> Love makes your soul crawl out from its hiding place.

~ **Zora Neale Hurston** *(1891-1960)*
Wrote 'Their Eyes Were Watching God' in 1937

> Healing begins where the wound was made.

~ **Alice Walker** *(1944)*
Author, well-known for her work as a social activist

> The greatest lie I ever told about love is that it sets you free.

~ Zadie Smith *(1975)*
English novelist, essayist, short story writer, a tenured professor in
the Creative Writing faculty of New York University since 2010

> It is not the size of the man, but the size of his heart that matters.

~ Evander Holyfield *(1962)*
Remains the only boxer in history to win the undisputed championship
in two weight categories: cruiserweight and heavyweight

> Think Black love, think universal love. Just think love.

~ Lauryn Hill *(1975)*
Her first solo album 'The Miseducation of Lauryn Hill,'
won many awards and broke several sales records

> If you can't love yourself how in the hell are you gonna love somebody else?

~ RuPaul *(1960)*
American drag queen, actor, model, singer, songwriter, television
personality who has won six Primetime Emmy Awards for
his reality competition series 'RuPaul's Drag Race'

> You can't build anything on a flimsy foundation. Friendship is the foundation.

~ Hill Harper *(1966)*
Won the NAACP Image Award for Outstanding Actor in a Drama
Series for three consecutive years for his role in "CSI: NY

> Men who are proud of being Black marry Black women; women who are proud of being Black marry Black men.

~ Malcolm X *(1925-1965)*
A popular figure during the civil rights movement. Assassinated in 1965

➤ All I'm saying is like, spoil me with your consistency. Always remain the same you and you won't have to worry about a different me.

~ **Wale** *(1984)*
Won BET Award for Best Collaboration in 2012
for the song 'Lotus Flower Bomb'

➤ Don't let your emotions overpower your intelligence.

~ **T.I.** *(1980)*
His original stage name T.I.P. stems from his childhood
nickname of "Tip" given to him by his grandfather and he
later changed to T.I. out of respect for label mate Q-Tip

➤ I have learned not to worry about love; but to honor its coming with all my heart.

~ **Alice Walker** *(1944)*
Showcased a bright mind at her segregated schools,
graduating from High School as class valedictorian

➤ Hate is only a form of love that hasn't found a way to express itself logically.

~ **Lil Wayne** *(1982)*
American rapper, singer, songwriter, record executive, entrepreneur, actor

➤ The times may have changed, but the people are still the same. We're still looking for love, and that will always be our struggle as human beings.

~ **Halle Berry** *(1966)*
American actress, won the Academy Award for Best Actress for 'Monster's
Ball,' becoming the only African American to have won the award

➤ The game isn't about chasing women … it's about getting yourself to a level where you are chosen by women.

~ **Tariq Nasheed** *(1974)*
American film producer, media personality, author

➤ What's better than followers, is actually falling in love.

~ **Chance the Rapper** *(1993)*
American rapper, singer, songwriter, actor, social activist

➤ You're my downfall, you're my muse, my worst distraction, my rhythm, and blues.

~ **John Legend** *(1978)*
American singer, songwriter, producer, actor, philanthropist, won an Academy Award for Best Original Song, 'Glory'

➤ Others may come and they will go. But I love you young and I'll love you old.

~ **Chaka Khan** *(1953)*
American singer, songwriter, lead vocalist of the funk band Rufus

➤ One thing that's true is that whether you are making a financial investment or an investment of the heart, you usually get what you give. What's also true is that investing the wrong assets into the wrong places is a great way to end up broke (or broken).

~ **Dr. Boyce Watkins** *(1971)*
American author, economist, political analyst, social commentator

➤ Some people don't even recognize real love when it comes without being called or sought.

~ **J. California Cooper** *(1931-2014)*
American playwright, author, named Black Playwright of the Year in 1978 for her play 'Strangers'

➤ What's the point in having it all without the person you love?

~ **Alicia Keys** *(1981)*
Was signed at 15 years old by Columbia Records

➢ There are Black men who are madly in love with White women. God bless them if that's what works for them. I just hope that we can strike a balance that portrays Black folks and the Black family in a light that's not extreme. Those are the types of characters I find myself attracted to.

~ Nia Long *(1970)*
American actress, producer

➢ Love, through all the ups and downs and joys and hurts. Love, for better or worse I still will choose you first.

~ Musiq Soulchild *(1977)*
American singer, songwriter

➢ I wish I could take what I'm feeling right now and put it in the water system, and we would all love each other.

~ Jamie Foxx *(1967)*
American actor, singer, comedian, songwriter, producer,
won an Academy Award for Best Actor in 'Ray'

➢ There's nowhere to hide when love is calling your name from the dark. Nowhere to run. There's nowhere to hide so let love have its way with your heart when love calls your name.

~ Kem *(1969)*
American R&B/Soul singer, songwriter, producer

➢ You can't have relationships with other people until you give birth to yourself.

~ Sonia Sanchez *(1934)*
Has authored over a dozen books of poetry, as well as short
stories, critical essays, plays, and children's books

➢ I love you takes 3 seconds to say, 3 hours to explain, and a lifetime to prove.

~ Reverend Run *(1964)*
One of the founding members of the influential rap group RUN-D.M.C.

➢ All you need in the world is love and laughter. That's all anybody needs. To have love in one hand and laughter in the other.

~ **August Wilson** *(1945-2005)*
American playwright, received two Pulitzer Prizes for Drama

➢ I could do this many ways, but I'ma fall fast and die with you.

~ **Lonr**
Artist, producer, songwriter

➢ Darkness cannot drive out darkness, only light can do that. Hate cannot drive out hate, only love can do that.

~ **Dr. Martin Luther King, Jr.** *(1929-1968)*
Between 1957 and 1968, he traveled over six million miles and spoke over twenty-five hundred times, appearing wherever there was injustice, protest, and action

➢ We hurt people that love us, love people that hurt us.

~ **Kendrick Lamar** *(1987)*
Regarded by many critics and contemporaries as one of the most influential hip-hop artists of his generation

➢ Some say we are responsible for those we love. Others know we are responsible for those who love us.

~ **Nikki Giovanni** *(1943)*
In 1967, she established Cincinnati's first ever Black Arts Festival

➢ Love yourself instead of loving the idea of other people loving you.

~ **Unknown**

CHAPTER 10

On Reality

What can I say about reality that is not already perfectly obvious? Reality bites, right? Wrong. Reality is simply the way things *really* are and not your idealized notion of how things are. Does that make sense to you? I know it does, but you would rather live the idealized version of your life, wouldn't you? Well, you can't!

To learn about yourself, you must walk through life awake with a clear vision of who you are and who you are not, what you must and must not do, where you are and are not going, when you are and are not doing the right thing, and why you are or are not fighting your own reality. It will help you navigate the world with clarity and a sense of direction.

You may be caught up in the monotony of life, living as you have always lived, accepting what you have always accepted, and disliking the place you are at. Then you may start something new, beat that horse dead, and still end up unhappy. What you have done is created a new monotony. A new reality that you are unhappy with because you cannot run away from yourself or your reality. What you must do is grow, evolve, and change so that your fantasy of reality can more closely match your actual reality.

The reality of the plight of Black men and women in America at the hands of the police grows more tragic as the death toll continues to rise across the country. Deriving from the need for major change against the systemic racism and violence toward Black people, the Black Lives Matter movement shed a spotlight on its pervasiveness in a way that seemed to open many eyes to the truth of "justice" for Black people in America.

The movement seemed to intimidate other races and the police alike, because we were finally standing up as a people and saying, "Look at us. We are here, and we matter too." Of course that is something that should be a given. We were not saying that *they* didn't matter. You see, they made it about them when it was about the importance of our mere existence, which has been overlooked throughout history. For me, the movement does not negate the lives of others. Rather, it stands firmly on the intrinsic value of Black lives, which seems not to factor in American society.

The brutal killings of Black men and women in our communities by police officers and citizens needed to be brought to the forefront, fought against, and changed. I do not believe the movement was born out of hatred of the police or of other races. It was born out of the need for equal justice under the law, accountability, proper protocol, human decency, and the concern for the mortality of Black lives.

Yes, all lives matter. But we Black people started seeing our reality too frequently play out violently in these streets, and nothing was being done to address the issue. It was abundantly clear that no one in power thought it was important enough to bring about a change of these heinous realities. Much like the civil rights movement, Black Lives Matter reminded Black people that we, too, deserve to be treated fairly, decently, justly, and with respect. We are also guaranteed equal treatment under the law. Our reality was not reflecting that, and a much-needed movement was born to manifest a new reality for all Black people across the globe.

If your life isn't what you want it to be, create a movement for yourself. Create positive change in your world so that you are empowered by living in your truth—the actual truth—and over time your reality will reflect your diligence. If you do not like what you see, do something about it. Go hard. Do it for yourself. Walk the walk, and your reality will evolve into, and quite possibly exceed, the fantasy you are living in.

If reality bites for you, take the time to discover the steps that evoke change and implement them. Be consistent, keep your nose to the grindstone, and make it happen for yourself. If the picture does not turn out the way you envisioned, do not fret. You are still making progress. You may simply have to change the path you are taking. Keep pressing forward, and do not stop until the reality you want is the reality you are living.

<u>On Reality</u>

➤ Your reality is yours, stop wasting time looking at someone else's reality while doing nothing about yours.

~ Steve Harvey *(1957)*
Radio and television host who has also written relationship advice books

➤ How far you go in life depends on your being tender with the young, compassionate with the aged, sympathetic with the striving, and tolerant of the weak and strong. Because someday in your life you will have been all of these.

~ George Washington Carver *(1860's-1943)*
The most prominent Black scientist of the early 20th century

➤ It is easier to build strong children than to repair broken men.

~ Frederick Douglass *(1818-1895)*
Became one of the most famous intellectuals of his time, lecturing to thousands on a range of causes, including women's rights

➤ If the Negro in the ghetto must eternally be fed by the hand that pushes him into the ghetto, he will never become strong enough to get out of the ghetto.

~ Carter G. Woodson *(1875-1950)*
Founder of the Study of African American Life and History, was one of the first scholars to study the history of the African diaspora, including African American history

➤ Some people are so poor, all they have is money.

~ Chance the Rapper *(1993)*
His third mix-tape, 'Coloring Book,' earned him three Grammy Awards, including the award for Best Rap Album, becoming the first streaming-only album to win a Grammy Award

➢ If Black lives mattered, I believe that policing and immigration enforcement would not be the devastating force that is in our communities.

~ **Opal Tometi** *(1984)*
Co-founder of Black Lives Matter

➢ The systems broken; the schools closed; the prisons open.

~ **Kanye West** *(1977)*
American rapper, record producer, fashion designer, had eight solo albums debuting at number one and 21 Grammy Awards, more than any other rapper

➢ Why is it that, as a culture, we are more comfortable seeing two men holding guns than holding hands?

~ **Ernest J. Gaines** *(1933-2019)*
American author whose works have been taught in college classrooms and translated into many languages

➢ I don't worry about the problem. I worry about the solution.

~ **Shaquille O'Neal** *(1972)*
American former professional basketball player who is a sports analyst on the TV program 'Inside the NBA,' widely considered one of the greatest players in NBA history

➢ Life doesn't stop because something happens to you.

~ **Magic Johnson** *(1959)*
After his retirement from basketball, he became an extremely successful entrepreneur, in 2012 he was a part of an ownership group that purchased the Los Angeles Dodgers

➢ My humanity is bound up in yours, for we can only be human together.

~ **Desmond TuTu** *(1931)*
Known for his work as an anti-apartheid activist, human rights activist

➢ Sometimes I have to remind myself that on my worst day I live like somebody on their greatest.

~ Meek Mill *(1987)*
American rapper, songwriter, activist

➢ It isn't where you came from, it's where you're going that counts.

~ Ella Fitzgerald *(1917-1996)*
American Jazz singer

➢ But to make a long story short, I need a shoulder 'cause the devil's on one, the other one I'm looking over.

Lil Wayne *(1982)*
Became one of the top-selling artists in hip-hop in the early 21ˢᵗ century, in 2009, he took home Grammy Awards for Best Rap Album, Best Rap Song, Best Rap Solo Performance, and Best Rap Performance by a Duo or Group

➢ When people don't want the best for you, they are not the best for you.

~ Gayle King *(1954)*
American television personality, author, broadcast journalist for CBS News, editor-at-large for O, The Oprah Magazine

➢ No person is your friend who demands your silence or denies your right to grow.

~ Alice Walker *(1944)*
Won the National Book Award for hardcover fiction for 'The Color Purple'

➢ If you are fortunate to have opportunity, it is your duty to make sure other people have those opportunities.

~ Kamala Harris *(1964)*
American attorney, U.S. Senator, Democratic Vice-Presidential candidate

➤ I knew then and I know now, when it comes to justice, there is no easy way to get it.

~ Claudette Colvin *(1939)*
American retired Nurse's Aide who was a pioneer
of the 1950's civil rights movement

➤ Every Colored person ain't dumb and all Whites are not racist. I be judging by the mind and heart, I ain't really into faces.

~ Lil Baby *(1994)*
Atlanta-bred rapper who quickly rose to fame after he launched his career
in 2017, following a series of mixtapes his career exploded in 2018

➤ You're not to be so blind with patriotism that you can't face reality. Wrong is wrong, no matter who does it or says it.

~ Malcolm X *(1925-1965)*
A popular figure during the civil rights movement. Assassinated in 1965

➤ True heroism is remarkably sober, very undramatic. It is not the urge to surpass all others at whatever cost, but the urge to serve others at whatever cost.

~ Arthur Ashe *(1943-1993)*
American professional tennis player who won 3 grand slam singles titles

➤ Men simply copied the realities of their hearts when they built prison. They simply extended into objective reality what was already a subjective reality. Only jailers believe in prison.

~ Richard Wright *(1908-1960)*
American author of novels, short stories, poems, and non-
fiction especially related to the plight of African Americans
during the late 19th to mid-20th centuries

➤ It's no disgrace to be Black, but it's often inconvenient.

~ James Weldon Johnson *(1871-1938)*
American author, civil rights activist, was a leader of the National Association
for the Advancement of Colored People, where he started working in 1917

➤ We are clear that all lives matter, but we live in a world where that's not actually happening in practice.

~ **Alicia Garza** *(1981)*
American civil rights activist, editorial writer, co-founder of the Black Lives Matter movement

➤ If we are going to be part of the solution, we have to engage in the problems.

~ **Majora Carter** *(1966)*
American urban revitalization strategist, public radio host

➤ You can't rely on how you look to sustain you, what sustains us, what is fundamentally beautiful is compassion; for yourself and for those around you.

~ **Lupida Nyong'o** *(1983)*
International filmmaker and actress known for her Academy Award winning role as Patsey in '12 Years a Slave'

➤ Make sure you are safe, and never put yourself in a compromising situation, but once that is checked off the list, I think it's really important for us to remember that someone needs us.

~ **Meghan Markle** *(1981)*
Duchess of Sussex, American actress

➤ I don't know what tomorrow holds. None of us do. We got to wait and see what God has planned.

~ **Roy Jones, Jr.** *(1969)*
American-born former professional boxer, boxing commentator, boxing trainer, rapper, actor who holds dual American and Russian citizenship

➤ Just because someone doesn't understand doesn't mean they don't want to.

~ **Regina King** *(1971)*
American actress, director, recipient of an Academy Award, Golden Globe and three Prime Time Emmy's, Time Magazine recognized her as one of the 100 most influential people in the world in 2019

➢ Like books and Black lives, albums still matter.

~ Prince *(1958-2016)*
American singer, songwriter, musician, record producer, dancer, actor, filmmaker

➢ Too many people spend money they haven't earned, to buy things they don't want, to impress people they don't like.

~ Will Smith *(1968)*
Transitioned from a successful rapper to a Hollywood A-lister

➢ Sometimes you got to hurt something to help something. Sometimes you have to plow under one thing in order for something else to grow.

~ Ernest J. Gaines *(1933-2019)*
His fiction, as exemplified by 'The Autobiography of Miss Jane Pitman'
and 'A Lesson Before Dying' reflects the African American experience

➢ Early is on time, on time is late, and late is unacceptable.

~ Eric Jerome Dickey *(1961)*
NY Times bestselling American author known for his
novels about contemporary African American life

➢ I certainly believe that being in contact with one's spirit and nurturing one's spirit is as important as nurturing one's body and mind. We are three dimensional beings: body, mind, spirit.

~ Laurence Fishburne *(1961)*
American actor, playwright, producer, screenwriter, film director

➢ Do not get lost in a sea of despair. Our struggle is not the struggle of a day, a week, a month, or a year, it is the struggle of a lifetime. Never ever be afraid to make some noise and get in good trouble, necessary trouble.

~ John Lewis *(1940-2020)*
American politician, civil rights leader, served in the United States
House of Representatives for Georgia from 1987 until his death

➤ People are going to judge you no matter what you do … don't worry about other people. Worry about you.

~ **Jacqueline Woodson** *(1963)*
American writer of books for children and adolescents

➤ There's the phrase of 'Making America Great Again,' but how did we make America great? Who did it? It was Thurgood Marshall who made America live up to its constitution, its dream. He pushed the envelope to make sure we were equal.

~ **Chadwick Boseman** *(1976-2020)*
American actor, his breakthrough performance came as baseball player Jackie Robinson in the biographical film '42' in 2013, also known for his portrayal of T'Challa/Black Panther

➤ There's a lot of people out there who go through hard times, and they feel alone. They feel like nobody is there. But I'm in the same boat.

~ **Brandy** *(1979)*
American singer, songwriter, record producer, actress, businesswoman

➤ And, to help society at large to understand that in the equation of life, fathers are of equal importance as mothers.

~ **Malik Yoba** *(1967)*
American actor, singer

CHAPTER 11

On Success

Success is subjective. Not all individuals have grandiose dreams for their lives. Some people are satisfied with the status quo. Others desire simple or minimalistic lifestyles. Some people live for money. Some live for love. Others for happiness. Success is relative to the lives of each of us.

It is not fair to judge success solely on monetary wealth. There is wealth in character. There is wealth in knowledge. There is wealth in self-love. There is wealth in happiness. Monetary wealth can buy you luxuries, but it cannot make you happy from within. Nor does it necessarily signify success. Some of the most miserable people I know are quite wealthy, yet they are not enjoyable to be around, and they do not seem to be happy in their lives. Is money worth the lack of personal satisfaction I presume they are experiencing?

We all want to have successful lives. We would also like to be able to live comfortably. My questions are, does success build character, or does character build success? Is success about wealth, or is success about character?

I do not know if I am objective enough to write on this topic. You see, I do have lofty goals and dreams for my life, but they are not wealth-based. They are based on love, friendship, happiness, security, loyalty, inspiration, and passion. All seven components must be present in my everyday world in order for me to function at my highest level. This is not an easy combination to maneuver daily, but I work at it like it is my job in order for my dreams to come true, thus leading to my success. I would like my success to lead to stability, not necessarily wealth. I would like a peaceful and loving existence with a partner, a close relationship with my family, financial stability, and a passionate freedom to pursue all my personal and business endeavors.

I believe that character builds wealth, and what that wealth is defined as depends on the values of the individual. Maybe money is what some people need to mask what else is missing in their worlds. For others, money may be what makes the world go around. For some, their self-esteem may be so low that wealth *does* build their character. Maybe happy does not even factor into the lives of many figuring they can buy their happiness. There are too many variables to calculate.

I believe that if we, as a Black community, stopped infighting and banded together to formulate business ventures, residential cooperatives, childcare facilities, employment opportunities, environmental responsibility in our neighborhoods, self-focused care, and success-motivated actions, not only would we build our characters but we would create wealth within our own communities. This is the type of wealth that is important to pass down to the next generation so that they can pass it down to the next generation. Generational wealth is what is needed to compete with the years of oppression we have experienced.

Individual wealth that is not shared and multiplied in a civic-minded way is just that—individual wealth. I get that we have to look after ourselves first, but to be selfish in the distribution of individual wealth is not helpful. Nor does it make you successful. It not only takes a village to raise a child, it takes a village to build widespread generational wealth. When our communities become successful, so will the people in those communities. I believe we should stop thinking of ourselves so much and think of the collective. The change that it would make in our communities would be life-altering for the rich and the poor alike.

The single mother raising her children alone in a positive, progressive way is successful regardless of her financial status. The college student working multiple jobs and sleeping on a futon to pay for his own tuition is successful regardless of his struggle. The felon who finally found a job as a busboy in a restaurant for minimum wage and is barely getting by is successful regardless of his past. What all these people have in common is the character and fortitude not to become victims of their circumstances and push forward, against all odds, to better themselves and their lives. This is wealth of the spirit, heart, and mind. In my opinion, this is the most important type of success you can possess.

As I said earlier, success is subjective, and I cannot be objective about it. If you strive to be the best individual you can be, grab hold of someone's hand and pull him or her up to your level (whatever that level is), and share your knowledge, wealth, and success. Then we, as a people, will all prosper. We would not be alone in our struggle. We would all have someone's hand in ours, paying it forward to create a race of people who have fostered knowledge, success, individual wealth, and generational wealth for themselves and generations to come. All it takes is a hand up, not a handout. For me, that is the epitome of success.

On Success

➤ Success is to be measured not so much by the position that one has reached in life as by the obstacles which he has overcome while trying to succeed.

~ Booker T. Washington *(1856-1915)*
Born into slavery, he rose to become a leading African American intellectual of the 19th century, founding Tuskegee Normal and Industrial Institute (Now Tuskegee University) in 1881

➤ Climb the ladder to success escalator style.

~ Notorious B.I.G. *(1972-1997)*
His 1994 release 'Ready to Die' was certified platinum quickly and he was named MC of the Year at the 1995 Billboard Music Awards

➤ Teach success before teaching responsibility. Teach them to believe in themselves. Teach them to think, 'I'm not stupid.' No child wants to fail. Everyone wants to succeed.

~ Al Green *(1946)*
American singer, songwriter, record producer, known as 'The Reverend Al Green'

➤ Success doesn't just land in your lap. You have to work, work, work, work, and work some more.

~ Sean Combs *(1969)*
American rapper, singer, songwriter, record producer, entrepreneur, record executive, actor

➤ He who is not courageous enough to take risks will accomplish nothing in life.

~ Muhammad Ali *(1942-2016)*
Widely regarded as one of the most significant and celebrated sports figures of the 20th century

➢ If you don't have confidence, you'll always find a way not to win.

> ~ **Carl Lewis** *(1961)*
> *American former track and field athlete who won 9 Olympic gold medals, 1*
> *silver medal and 10 World Championship medals, including 8 gold medals*

➢ Life has 2 rules: Number 1, never quit! Number 2, always remember rule number one.

> ~ **Duke Ellington** *(1899-1974)*
> *American composer, pianist, leader of a jazz orchestra*

➢ Success is not an accident. Success is actually a choice.

> ~ **Stephen Curry** *(1988)*
> *American professional basketball player, six-time NBA Allstar,*
> *won 3 NBA championships with the Golden State Warriors*

➢ Every day is a new opportunity to reach that goal.

> ~ **Rick Ross** *(1976)*
> *American rapper, songwriter, entrepreneur, record executive*

➢ Don't let anything stop you. There will be times when you'll be disappointed, but you can't stop.

> ~ **Sadie T. M. Alexander** *(1898-1989)*
> *First African American to receive a PhD in economics in the United States,*
> *the first woman to receive a law degree from the University of Pennsylvania*
> *Law School, first African American woman to practice law in Pennsylvania*

➢ If you know whence you came, there is really no limit to where you can go.

> ~ **James Baldwin** *(1924-1987)*
> *One of the 20th century's greatest writers, especially known*
> *for his essays on the Black experience in America*

➢ Success is about dedication. You may not be where you want to be or do what you want to do when you're on the journey, but you've got to be willing to have vision and foresight that leads you to an incredible end.

~ Usher *(1978)*
American singer, songwriter, actor, dancer

➢ Set your business plan to win; raise the bar or you're not going to be prepared. You need to think that what you're doing will make you $100 million.

~ Swizz Beatz *(1978)*
American hip-hop recording artist, DJ, record
producer, art collector, entrepreneur

➢ If you wake up deciding what you want to give versus what you're going to get, you become more successful. In other words, if you want to make money, you have to help someone else make money.

~ Russell Simmons *(1957)*
American entrepreneur, record executive, writer, film producer,
Chairman and CEO of Rush Communications, co-founder of
Def Jam Records, created the Phat Farm clothing fashion line

➢ The first revolution is when you change your mind.

~ Gil Scott-Heron *(1949-2011)*
American soul and jazz musician, author, known primarily for
his work as a spoken word performer in the 1970's and 80's

➢ Set your goals high, and don't stop until you get there.

~ Bo Jackson *(1962)*
American retired professional baseball and football player, the only
professional athlete in history to be named an All-Star in both
baseball and football, his elite talent in multiple sports has given
him the reputation as one of the greatest athletes of all time

➤ May the optimism of tomorrow be your foundation for today.

~ **Wale** *(1984)*
Rose to prominence in 2006 when his song 'Dig Dug (Shake It)' became popular in his hometown of Washington DC

➤ I have discovered in life that there are ways of getting almost anywhere you want to go if you really want to go.

~ **Langston Hughes** *(1902-1967)*
American poet, social activist, novelist, playwright, columnist

➤ Success doesn't come to you … you go to it.

~ **Marva Collins** *(1936-2015)*
Best known for creating Westside Preparatory School in 1975

➤ Start where you are, with what you have. Make something of it and never be satisfied.

~ **George Washington Carver** *(died 1943)*
The most prominent Black scientist of the 20th century

➤ Some people want it to happen, some wish it would happen, others make it happen.

~ **Michael Jordan** *(1963)*
Principal owner of the Charlotte Hornets

➤ One important key to success is self-confidence. An important key to self-confidence is preparation.

~ **Arthur Ashe** *(1943-1993)*
First Black tennis player selected to the U.S. Davis Cup Team, only Black man ever to win the singles title at Wimbledon, the U.S. Open and the Australian Open

➤ All business is personal … make your friends before you need them.

~ **Robert L. Johnson** *(1946)*
American entrepreneur, media magnate, executive,
philanthropist, investor, co-founder of BET

➤ If it's flipping hamburgers at McDonald's, be the best hamburger flipper in the world. Whatever it is you do you have to master your craft.

~ **Snoop Dogg** *(1971)*
American rapper, singer, songwriter, producer,
actor, media personality, entrepreneur

➤ Success is the result of perfection, hard work, learning from failure, loyalty, and persistence.

~ **Colin Powell** *(1937)*
American politician, retired four-star general in the United States Army,
served as the National Security Advisor, as Commander of the U.S.
Army Forces Command and as Chairman of the Joint Chiefs of Staff

➤ Instead of looking at the past, I put myself ahead twenty years and try to look at what I need to do now in order to get there then.

~ **Diana Ross** *(1944)*
Lead singer of the Supremes who became Motown's
most successful act in the 1960's

➤ Never chase money. You should chase success, because with success money follows.

~ **Wilfred Emmanuel-Jones** *(1957)*
British businessman, farmer, Founder of The
Black Farmer range of food products

➤ The difference between winners and losers is winners know exactly who they are and aren't scared to be authentic.

~ **Wendy Williams** *(1964)*
American television host, businesswoman, media
personality, author, radio DJ and host

➤ I believe in destiny. But I also believe that you can't just sit back and let destiny happen. A lot of times, an opportunity might fall into your lap, but you have to be ready for that opportunity. You can't sit there waiting on it. A lot of times you are going to have to get out there and make It happen.

~ **Spike Lee** *(1957)*
American film director, producer, writer, actor, professor

➤ Helping other people is the definition of success. The biggest effect you can have in life is that on the lives of others, and we should be afraid to die until we've made a major contribution to society.

~ **Rick Ross** *(1976)*
The first artist to be signed to P. Diddy's Ciroc Entertainment, he founded his own music label, Maybach Music Group, in 2009

➤ Wealth is not about having a lot of money; it's about having a lot of options.

~ **Chris Rock** *(1965)*
American comedian, actor, writer, producer, director

➤ Change happens from the bottom up – all of us as individuals deciding that we will, and we do have an impact.

~ **Hill Harper** *(1966)*
A full-time member of Boston's Black Folk's Theater Company, one of the nation's oldest and most respected African American traveling theater troupes

➤ In a world full of people, only some want to fly. Isn't that crazy?

~ **Seal** *(1963)*
British singer, songwriter

➤ I'd rather regret the risks that didn't work out than the chances I didn't take at all.

~ Simone Biles *(1997)*
American artistic gymnast, with a combined total of 30 Olympic and World Championship medals, she is the most decorated American gymnast and the world's third most decorated gymnast

➤ You wanna know what scares people? Success. When you don't make moves and when you don't climb up the ladder, everybody loves you because you're not competition.

~ Nicki Minaj *(1982)*
Trinidadian-American rapper, singer, songwriter, actress, model, entered the music business as a backup singer for local aspiring singers in New York City

➤ The only time you should look back in life is to see how far you have come.

~ Kevin Hart *(1979)*
American stand-up comedian, actor, producer

➤ I am no longer accepting the things I cannot change. I am changing the things I cannot accept.

~ Angela Y. Davis *(1944)*
American political activist, philosopher, academic, author